ARIK BERNSTEIN

THE ISRAELI SOCIAL DECLINE

A Look From Within

ISBN: 1500298379
ISBN-13: 9781500298371
Library of Congress Control Number: 2014911597
CreateSpace Independent Publishing Platform
North Charleston, South Carolina

Humbly do I beseech the forgiveness of God as well as that of my human brethren lest I wronged them through my ignorance and/or my bad traits.

TABLE OF CONTENTS

Preface · vii
Acknowledgments · xi

Chapter 1 The Corporation Society · 1
Chapter 2 For My Brothers' and Companions' Sake,
                 I Will Now Say… · 23
Chapter 3 The Hidden Trap of Samson's Option · · · · · · · · · · · · · 35
Chapter 4 Jewish State and the Arab-Israeli Conflict · · · · · · · · · 45
Chapter 5 Catalysts Causing the Further Loss of Values in Israel · · · 71
Chapter 6 Possible Solutions · 89
Chapter 7 The Elephant in the China Shop · · · · · · · · · · · · · 105
Chapter 8 And What If… · 113

Appendix A More about Various Sides of Zionism · · · · · · · · · · · 117
Appendix B The Way toward Reforms: Additional
                  Suggested Corrections · 121

PREFACE

It was the best of times, it was the worst of times, it was the age of wisdom, it was the age of foolishness, it was the epoch of belief, it was the epoch of incredulity, it was the season of Light, it was the season of Darkness, it was the spring of hope, it was the winter of despair, we had everything before us, we had nothing before us, we were all going direct to heaven, we were all going direct the other way.
—Charles Dickens, A Tale of Two Cities

This book was written during a time-out that lasted more than two years. I was compelled to take it due to my mother's deteriorating health. Old age is certainly not an enticing sight, yet during its advance, both the family and the elderly person can't help but confront the changing social world and its values (or might I say, a lack of values) concerning the aging process. The insights in this book were partially born through my observation of what was happening at my home as well as in the homes of others in regards to this painful process.

Perceptions and thoughts that had nested in my brain for a long time took wing while I guarded my mother and took care of her, particularly during the long sleepless nights, either at home or at the hospital. I kept thinking about the last conversations I held with my mother when she was still able to converse, conversations that touched on the world of her childhood values—values whose existence had evidently expired a long time ago. I asked myself about the loss of these values, which has caused the present state of the ethical and social situation in Israel. Is it the deficiency of one major value or perhaps the loss of several values that are not interrelated but are weighty enough significant enough to have created a serious situation that one cannot ignore?

The answers that came to my mind are presented in the chapters of this book, and I do hope that these may instigate some fresh thinking by the intelligent reader. I am aware that many of these questions are still, in many ways, unanswered, and apparently are waiting for me to gain courage and strength and undertake further profound research.

Initially, I wrote the chapters in the book as separate articles, as the first draft and basis for my doctoral paper. Like humans, so the environment around us also blooms and withers, either through natural periodicity or following the artificial one created by people. Global economic and social events, starting with demonstrations by youths in Spain and moving through the Occupy Wall Street movement and the Israeli Summer of Protest,[1] had a profound impact on my desire to research specific topics in political science. However, while I was writing my articles, the Arab Spring turned into a stormy winter, and most of the countries in the Middle East are now characterized by political instability. My articles suddenly lost their focal point, at which point I switched from pursuing research and scientific goals to focusing on the need to present my outlooks and thoughts and express my opinions in writing.

Originally, the articles were written in Hebrew, and the translation was meant for academic purposes only. However, after a while I started to work on the translated drafts, added descriptive expressions and

---

1   Occupy Wall Street is a people-powered movement that began on September 17, 2011, in Liberty Square and has spread to over fifteen hundred cities globally. The 2011 Israeli social justice protests were a series of demonstrations in Israel beginning in July 2011 involving hundreds of thousands of protesters from a variety of socioeconomic and religious backgrounds opposing the continuing rise in the cost of living (particularly housing) and the deterioration of public services, such as health and education. A common rallying cry at the demonstrations was the chant "The people demand social justice!" As the protests expanded during August 2011, the demonstrations also began to focus on other related issues relating to the social order and power structure in Israel. (Wikipedia, s.v. "2011 Israeli Social Justice Protests," last modified July 17, 2015. https://en.wikipedia.org/wiki/2011_Israeli_social_justice_protests)

statements, and excluded terms such as *paradigm* or *research query*. As part of this change in writing, almost all the references in my later paper were quoted from Wikipedia for the sake of simplicity and comprehension. I regard it as a good and accurate enough source for the intelligent reader, useful for expanding on and clarifying concepts that are normally beyond anyone's spheres of interest. At specific points, I used chosen terms for marked issues only and limited the scope of my explanations for those words. For example, I used the term *Sephardic* for Jews who came from Arabic countries, and the term *Mizrachi* for the Jewish people with religious-national ideas as per the Mizrachi movement. This is an explanation for those who do have some understanding of these terms; for most of my readers, who live far away from Israel, it shouldn't make a difference.

Despite the cohesive observations interwoven in my book, I was meticulous about separating the text into chapters based on the drafts of the articles I had written earlier, and I did preserve a separate internal structure for each chapter. Thus, most of the chapters include an introduction, description, and suggested solutions to the problems I present. I do hope that this method will make it easier for the reader who is interested in leafing through this book. On the other hand, this method should not prevent readers with proficiency in such matters from reading the book from cover to cover.

As a rule, this book takes its reader from the challenges that are mutual for Israelis and other nations around the world to those that are different and distinguish the Israeli-Jewish challenge from all others. My starting and unchanging opinion is that at present, the state of Israel is facing a social and moral crossroad of unprecedented importance. This situation is partly affected by the affluent global-society phenomenon, by global and multinational corporations, and by the age of consumption. Another part is affected by internal, imminent challenges of the Jewish people and the intricacies of the state due to its social structure and origins.

I do not argue here for an inclusive and absolute systemic vision. I find it difficult to see the field of social and moral quandaries as one mechanism that responds to all needs and difficult problems. The present book was constructed on the basis of my personal moral perceptions, which the reader is most likely to agree with but at the same time may also have reservations about.

With reference to that, I should probably reveal the fact that I am a conservative. I believe in God, and hence I find life to be a precious gift that should not be taken lightly by us humans. Therefore, I object to abortions (as long as there is no risk to the carrying mother), though I do oppose the use of violence or even legal means against it; instead, I promote forming an opinion through education and cultural persuasion. Obviously, I am against capital punishment based on the same reasoning. I don't appreciate governmental intervention in local affairs, and I am not persuaded by grand theories about equality and justice for all. It is not because I disagree with the notions expressed by such utopist thinkers, but rather by the way those wonderful ideas are very often translated by cynical leaders into a grim reality. In a nutshell, I don't trust revolutions and/or revolutionaries. As far as I am concerned, if social justice is supposed to side with the people, it should come from the people through a time-tested process, and not in any other way. Economically speaking, I am all for the gold standard, and I have my own suspicion that deviating from it caused many of the much of the poor economy we see nowadays.

Now it is over but not done with. I am turning to you, my readers, and I wish to let you know that I would be glad to receive your reactions and opinions. After all, each new insight begets yet another new awareness that grows from it, and I feel that as the writer in this case, I may be the greatest ignoramus of all.

—Ra'anana; Israel, September 2015

ACKNOWLEDGMENTS

This manuscript is dedicated to the memory of the breathtaking love shared between my dear deceased father, Izzy Bernstein, and my dear long-lived mother, Lucy Bernstein.

I owe a special gratitude to my sister-in-law, Isabella Arad, for helping me with the early translations and editing of the initial versions of this document. I guess thanks are in order also to my brother's sons, Yonatan and Avichai, for teasing their old uncle one too many times, one should hope.

CHAPTER 1:

THE CORPORATION SOCIETY

*Wild Capitalism, or the Reign of the Few through
the Corporate Regime*

*Seven Deadly Sins
Wealth without work
Pleasure without conscience
Science without humanity
Knowledge without character
Politics without principle
Commerce without morality
Worship without sacrifice.*
—Mahatma Gandhi

Introduction

Please be advised again that my perceptions are conservative, so I do not
readily accept doctrines that are imposed upon me from above—ideals
from this or that world of ideas to which one is supposed to aspire. In
that aspect, I find in our basic beliefs sufficient moral ground for guidance. Hence, it is clear that I do not side with communist revolutions,
and, as I have mentioned only a page or two ago, as a rule I have reservations about revolutions and revolutionaries per se.

To my joy, I have been lucky to live in a time of victory over commu-
nism and its many evils; however, on the opposite side, in the darkness,

a different threat has developed and thrived. Sometimes we do not have to be cautious about the familiar enemy but rather about the one that crawls in the darkness of our own backyards and turns our world into a turbid one.

During recent times—and by that I refer mainly to the period from the middle of the twentieth century to the present time—a perception has gradually spread all over the world: the perception of boundless capitalism that sanctifies consumption and avoids the depth of thought that is an integral part of my desirable world's picture. That malady has spread all around the globe and is affecting the lives of billions.

The detachment of the US currency's value from the gold standard (the Nixon Shock[2]) transmitted a speculative message throughout the entire capitalist system. Now it is possible to accumulate wealth "on paper" regardless of the financial reality, if one is sufficiently creative on the one hand and lacking conscience or social values on the other.

In this insane atmosphere, old and new international corporations have allowed their wealthy owners to avoid paying taxes while they accumulate perquisites in the many countries that cry out for economic investment and inducement so that their own economic systems may flourish. Thus, a thin worldwide social layer has evolved consisting of owners and high executives who jointly share the greatest economic wealth and power ever seen in the hands of few. In Israel, this social layer does not include more than several hundred people.

After a giant corporation has joined the national economy, the local commercial and financial systems become predisposed in its favor. Each contractor's company working with that corporation is committed to its rules regarding profit margins as well as its morality regarding payment. On the surface, everyone may seem happy with this situation. But what happens when we examine the quality of the product or test

---

2 The Nixon Shock was a series of economic measures undertaken by United States President Richard Nixon in 1971, the most significant of which was the unilateral cancellation of the direct convertibility of the United States dollar to gold. (Wikipedia, s.v. "Nixon Shock," last modified July 6, 2015, https://en.wikipedia.org/wiki/Nixon_Shock)

its durability? What about the contractor's workers and their economic state? What about the workers' salaries and living conditions?

I believe it is in the best interest of each human society, wherever it exists, to have specific and critical numbers of people with the financial capability to develop their streets and neighborhoods. This group of people consists of small dealers who are, in fact, the bread and butter of the capitalist system as well as of the representative democracy, for they care about the appearance of the pavement in front of their stores as well as the tidiness of their streets. This social class is the one interested in parking places and accessibility to the center of town; it's the petty bourgeoisie, in which ideas and needs are perpetually concocted, so they can be turned into economic action and political impulses that support and subsist off those employees living in the surrounding neighborhood or city. They make enough money to afford a little more than their basic necessities.

Again, the temptation of the short-sighted politician to see the economy reinforced by the international corporation leads to perquisites for that corporation, which in turn favors the corporation during the uneven competition that forms within the economy. The first ones harmed are small businesses, which lose their usual narrow margins of profits because they cannot compete with a corporation that sells cheap goods in great quantities. The combination of "cheap" and "great quantities" leads to the decrease of profits that are normally expected: on the one hand at the expense of the employees' salaries, and on the other hand at the expense of the product's quality in the course of time.

One of the proven ways to sell a product is to increase quantity at the expense of durability. When customers keep products for a long time, this prevents new products from entering the market. The income of the employee and the profit for the small business and its owner decreases, as does any political power the individual may have. Because of a lack of funds, the individual cannot contribute financially or even offer some of their free time to the political system to help affect a change. Small-business owners can't even contemplate competing with the corporation due to its size; the rules of the game are already in the corporation's favor. After there is an immediate threat by the big firms in the economy—meaning "if they do not want us (i.e., the corporation), we can always leave"—the inevitable outcome is submission of the political leadership to the might of the corporation, resulting in decrease of worker salaries or an increase in unemployment. One consonant doesn't seem to change; in time, an overall slow decrease appears in the state's revenues from commerce and taxes.

At present, there are corporations that wield even greater economic power than their respective governments. These corporations are interested in the continuation of the national-governmental method and are looking for a way they can continue to pull the governmental strings without being visible targets. They apply pressure by making contributions to election campaigns, constructing industrial plants in various territories as means for regional development, reinforcing alternative employment possibilities, and so on.

Systemic Paralysis

Capital-rule relations, as part of the chosen establishment's inability to provide protection for the simple citizen, are rewarded and encouraged by the lust for profit of the leaders and the administrative class (namely, assuring lucrative future positions for present politicians and government officials). In Israel, the influential leader's arena is decreased because of the 120-member house of parliament.[3] An interesting situation has evolved in which the state discards social services and welfare services (including legal bills concerning prisons and various kinds of policing) and transfers their operation to fellowships, organizations, and private groups; yet the state still demands the same loyalty as it did when the state delivered such services to its citizens.

Through private agents, corporations take over services that the state has given up, such as unemployment, prison, or police services.

---

3 The *Knesset* (literally *the gathering*) is the unicameral national legislature of Israel.

4

Beyond that, the corporations also take control of the civilian society and nonprofit charity organizations under the pretense of "contribution to the social and civilian agenda." At the same time, corporations complete their control, as well as ownership rights, over much of the communication media, advertising companies, and public relations companies and are thus, starting from that point, in control over the entire scope of any public debate. There is a coordinated voice—though it may not be easily noticed—of the corporation in the public sphere. Throughout it all, the corporation's tremendous power is concealed, and it seems as though the state and its branches are the ones running the show.

It is easy for states to ignore economic transgressions by corporations when a weak and helpless police force, as well as other law enforcement authorities that do not protect the citizen from harm and crime, are combined with paralyzed advocacy. this state of affairs encourages creative accounting, which is not supervised by higher echelons of the state. A good symptom of this malady is that when criminal organizations reach the level of business, their next step is to find a way to join forces with the corporations. Then, usually after a realization period, there is an apparent decline in the voter turnout, which illustrates the citizens' lack of trust in their ability to have an impact, as well as the workers' unions decreased capability to act on their own behalf. All of these developments are parts of the merciless capitalism in which all of the citizens' representatives are simply disappointing and do not protect them anymore. The courthouses are costly and overloaded; the arbitration system is biased due to the "weight" of the competitor. Not only is the court's writ-of-execution system not functioning, but it sometimes collaborates with underworld organizations, which may be "bought" by or join hands with the big corporations.

In the future, when corporations stop hiding behind the local governments, people may be forced to face a situation in which the corporations they work for determine the level of citizenship they are entitled to, including the level of justice and the law. A similar situation already existed during the Middle Ages for those who were part of the clergy class.

The church acted as a state within a state and operated separate systems of justice and law, as well as a different system of codes and norms for its members. The regular laws of the kingdom did not apply to the clergy class, and there was no state authority that could impose the rules of the kingdom on them. Even regarding enforcement, they were only subservient to the soldiers and army of the Pope, present in many Christian states. These rules were then accepted by some of the realms of Europe, in accordance with their local laws and agreements with the Vatican.

In a futuristic corporate world, the meaning of such rules would not be less comprehensive, but it would be a manifold one at the beginning, for it would concern much more than only one corporation. Only with the decadence and fall of the corporate method, the number of corporations could diminish until only one remains.

Damage to the Social Texture

The Internet is regarded as a useful tool for the young generation and for freedom fighters everywhere, but it can also play to the hand of the corporations. The World Wide Web has the ability to harm social cohesion because it has promoted paranoia and alienation between neighbors. Screens consist of actual physical separation (no more-or-less talking to your neighbor along the fences; and due to the nonjudgmental side of the Internet, there is less ability to evaluate people for who they really are). Therefore, people in the community become more apprehensive, introverted, and scared. They feel that their human environment is hostile and, to care for the state of the communality within it, is pushed aside due to the need for present personal status and a desirable self-image in such environment. The corporations are also not interested in the existence of deep relationships among the community's members. Such relations may, for example, lead them to form trade unions; they may also lead to the development of tastes and wishes, among the employees, that require substantial financial investment on the part of the corporation in order to match the end products to the wild and diverse fashions that emerge from the different communities. Instead, corporations prefer that community members have only superficial contacts and rely upon corporate materialism to create goods and a sense of happiness. This false happiness, which was concocted in the PR branch of the corporation, may provide according to the point of view of the corporation enough basis and incentives among community members to follow these lines. What the corporations actually produce must be delivered to the public by either the corporations themselves or by reality easy-to-bend celebrities, as yet another symbol of how corporations influence the thought processes of the masses.

Just as in-depth relations (among society members) are unwanted by the corporations, so too is the institution of extended family, for it seems to support refuge for the individual and a kind of shelter against the long arm of the corporation. Consider, for example, a young family member who owns a small grocery shop next to a 7-Eleven mini-mart. His parents might support his efforts by offering him free lodging in their home, thus cutting his personal expenses and freeing up his cash to put back into his business. Due to historic and developmental reasons, it is difficult to turn the nucleus family into a good target for public bashing. Instead, corporations may support alternative families, such as single parent, because as a rule this enables the weakening of important connections among more traditional and usually more economically settled families. It should be stressed that the alternative kinds of connections are worthy of existence in their own right, and the fact that they are flourishing is not related to the corporation. Nevertheless, in my eyes, their introduction as competition for the traditional family is done consciously to weaken all family relations in society.

Seemingly, the corporation contributes to the community but prefers to take over the place of the community or supposedly lead it to help the needy and the poor. In the past, such charitable activity stemmed from community empathy, whereas currently it is supposedly led by the corporation. So to summaries this section, without the corporation, the individual cannot have material status in the community, cannot make progress at work, and cannot define his or her self. The link to the ethos of accessible cheap goods that is invented by the corporation early on destroys any possibility of the individual bequeathing long-lasting material goods to his or her children.

Conceptual Change

During the transformation of the powers between the state and the corporation, an ideological perception that concentrates on the human status according to branded property takes the place of the old ideologies. It does not matter if your house is good and your roof is not leaking. What matters is that your family members are dressed according to the latest fashion, one in a series of everlasting passing fashions. In such a world, a long-lasting product has no meaning because, in any case, the fashion will change by the end of the month and the status of the product's owners will be measured by their proximity to the latest fashion. That is why products are not manufactured to last long, or alternatively, durability is becoming the least-important consideration in goods desirability. The act of manufacturing products that are not built to last does not meet the absolute needs of the consumer/citizen, but is most useful for the corporations. That is, they have found a way to earn more money based not on the quality of the product in the long run, but on its cultural and social trends for a limited time. Clearly, private media periodically assist the corporations by glorifying changes of fashion; however, if you are not part of the upper social layer that manages these corporations, which you likely are not, due to the concentration of its capital in the hands of few, this situation provides you, the simple person, with minimal security in what you purchase and in your current occupation (fashions do change). Hence, it makes a simple person's values in life redundant, and in exchange promises him or her only a slight chance of economic leisure (a break from the buying race) or success (similar to the chances of winning the lottery).

This is a distortion of capitalism, which prevents individuals from having truly free initiatives and intensifies the power of money and property as more important than morals or merit. Thus, knowledge is not considered important unless it is of practical use in the interest of the new economy. This undervaluation of knowledge, in turn, has caused the decline of the humanities and theoretical sciences.

It's interesting to observe how two different individuals with contrary set of believes still manage to fall into the same trap.

Conservatives…whereas they preserve old values of morality and mutual familial and community help, they are perceived as reactionaries in the eyes of society…sometimes even in their own eyes. Seemingly, they are detached from reality because they focus on old formulas of life and not on what is most important at the time, that being money and shopping lists. Some conservatives become desperate and turn into bitter or extremist individuals.

The fall of liberals into the same trap is a little more refined. Their basic assumption is that it is possible to introduce reactionary changes into society by bringing down social improvements from the upper layer to the lower one (e.g., from the intellectual class to the masses), when these measures are accompanied by appropriate legislation and educational changes. Thus, it is possible to persuade liberals that the changes in our consumption and cloture by the corporations are part of the sanctification of modernity and part of scientific and technological progress. Indeed, the change from an old washing machine with out-of-date technology to one that functions with air bubbles, or from medium-sized cell-phone screens to the bigger ones, may be perceived as technological change with repercussions on the length and quality of our leisure-time activities. On the other hand, the change may be considered as trivial, which leads to the challenge of how one can build the "buzz" around the trendiness in such imagined progress.

The International Arena
As mentioned earlier in this chapter, the corporation in general, wherever it may have a branch, has no interest in causing the state to collapse, for it

serves as a perfect cover added by the true motivations and interests that run our governmental process. On the one hand, there is the obvious financial influence of the corporation on the political candidates for governmental positions before and after their tenure. On the other hand, corporate lawyers and professionals ensure the bending and weakening of the rule of law by finding flaws and delays in every legal procedure. Lawyers may even use pure bullying tactics to scare voters or community leaders (provided the leaders are considered sufficiently brave) with threats to cut future financial investments in their state or electoral region. An individual's livelihood depends on his or her employment, and that is why such financial "clamps" are very large and tight.

That is all well and good in the local arena; however, the corporation is mostly interested in keeping the international arena decentralized so that it does not possess the vitality or power to stop the corporation from exploiting one's state vulnerability against the other on various financial and legal levels. Such exploitation is expressed through various levels of income that turn place A into one in which it is worthwhile to produce and turn place B into one suitable for sales or open to exploit international conflicts in order to enhance output and sales. (This is discerned particularly in the weapons industries.)

As a rule, any international arena that is divided and lacks legal and government-dominant leading powers serves as an open and free meadow without true supervision or real-time policing of the crimes and misconduct of the corporation.

The world media act as the leading unit in the corporation's world perception. For the corporation to control the consciousness of individuals and groups, it must control world communication and invent a global language that encourages the corporation's vision. However, what is the vision of the corporation if not lip service for the elite and, less so, for the masses? All of it is a public relations smoke screen camouflaging the will of the corporation's owners to gain power and resources.

Usually, the separate national armies play a fundamental role in the continuation of sales and the solution for the corporation's end profit issues. The problem is that the same system eventually requires some goods lessening, which means in plain language battle action. In the theater, the gun placed on the table in act one must eventually be used to shoot. Thus, this issue also has an answer, and it is latent in the profits of many corporations through the restoration following any major war.

National identity is mostly used by the local marketing department of many big corporations as a catalyst for profits during competitions with other nations. The worker's productivity in any competing nation enhances the corporation's production abilities worldwide, but one must not mention comparison of purchase abilities between the rivaling states unless one is on the "right" side of the national equation.

Private individuals do not have the global ability to compare their power as small dealers with the corporate power that might "choke" them; therefore, this is not a true competition. The only competition stems from the corporation's absorption ability, as it wishes to preserve its national and international incompetent façade. That is why national legislation will always enable the start-up success of the individual but will always help the existing global corporation purchase it later on.

Social Impact

Individuals at the head of each corporation collect most of the profits, and they act as cultural and social examples for others. They are courted by the media, which most likely is partly owned by them, and they invent new language and new ideas that fairly justify their separate existence opposite the different existence of other citizens.

It is that thin layer of corporate elite that turn into the backstage-ruling elite. By definition, the ruling class is impermeable with capabilities and strength that are not even given to verbal description. Members of this class are not the friends of the presidents; they are their creators! There is no information that is not available to them, and, to a great extent, they are the ones handling the supreme management of economics in global politics, which they direct in order to increase their profits and power. This does not insinuate that there is a conspiracy but rather a natural move of growth and flow of doings leading to the top of the pyramid and holding one's position while one is there.

Some sub-phenomenon tends to show on the social map when the distribution of wealth is so uneven. Once more, finances are concentrated in the hands of a few; there is a lack of money among other classes, mainly among the middle class. Its members then retreat from a socioeconomic perspective due to their inability to provide their children the same life-style to which they were accustomed when they were growing up.

When contractors realize that it is more profitable to build houses for the rich, the index for service prices increases, as does the price of apartments for the middle class and especially for young couples who evolved in that class. In such cases, the parents' generation might need to invest more money in their children's housing, which can endanger their own livelihoods in old age.

Another side effect relates to the actual habitation of these becoming expensive apartments. Due to the rise in home prices, sometimes extended family members may need to live together in the same house that previously accommodated the parents with their young children. One must not confuse this situation with communality, for this is the beginning of the decline toward the poverty line and not a return to the healthy communality of that social class.

At the end, a crowded living situation leads to an accelerated collapse of the infrastructures (such as overused water supply and over floated sewage tunnels) and to a vastly decreased quality of life. In some cases, there is an increase in related sicknesses. That is why the stress on the public system intensifies and why increasing taxes taken from the once wealthy people and remaining middle class cannot meaningfully change the once-middle classes and today's lower classes deteriorating reality. On the contrary, more people from the middle class will cross the lines to the poorer side of society. In most cases, members of the thin layer who control the corporations do not sense the difference, thanks to creative taxing and strong political lobbies. Presently the situation in many countries around the world is such that the middle-class communities are unable to support the weaker families among them who have reached a state of crisis. Everything that the welfare state is supposed to give—and which, according to the American myth, is given by the supporting community—cannot be actualized due to the community's poverty and the growing sense of alienation between neighbors.

When our security and livelihood depend on the economy of the big corporations, there is more of a sense of bitterness about our economic failure as individuals. During a certain period of the twentieth century, this bitterness was channeled to the modern coliseum, namely the television, and then as somewhat expected by many educators, it sprouted through the social rules of public and personal behavior in our own conduct toward our actual neighbors in the street or neighborhood. Under the impact of the twenty-first-century television and its reality shows where the outcome is either to "live or die," everything turns into a zero-sum game: Are you the last survivor on the island who won a million/the girl/the apartment or the vacation? In this kind of a world, the winners have no other desire but to be portrait as perfect and, as such, suitable for their dream world. The television show is like a pregnancy, at the end of which a dream child is born, or else there is no child at all. Under those cultural influences, it is my firm believe that the public violence and tension levels will increase, and the compassion for the weak will be interpreted as trivial weakness or luxury.

In such a violent world where the individual's security is so frayed, there is a naturally increased tendency to turn to the closest pertinent group for support in order to enhance the sensation of control.[4] In fact, the real control over our lives is taken away from us. The elite class in control is the one that fortifies its settlements with a growing number of police stations and private police forces. Small communities and towns with well-protected "gates" preventing the entry of strangers also prevent any possibility of social diffusion.

---

4 Groups such as hate groups, gangs, religious factions, and so forth.

Before I continue, let me emphasize again and again, as before, that *I do not side with any communist perception whatsoever.* What is stated here is the product of a very worried individual with a sturdy conservative vision.

In my view, we now live in a society that privatizes its humanity for the sake of economic profits that are harvested by the few. Capitalism is based on personal initiatives, hard work, and belief in the success of one's business; however, in a world in which the powerful ones dictate the rules of the game and are changing the ground rules according to their changing needs, there is no chance for heaps of new entrepreneurs. Only a few of them try to grow, and most of them fail, so their only solution is to sell their young businesses and ideas to the big companies. In fact, this is the modern equivalent to a death sentence for small businesses in older and newer industries, since they are unable to compete economically with the big corporations.

In the field of innovation—one of the last fields in the hands of small businesses and where the individual can still give a bit of competition—business owners are still forced at some point to sell their entrepreneurship to those who are bigger than they are. In fact, in a sophisticated social and perceivable manner, an everlasting hanging threat of bankruptcy is seemingly perceived as positive because it allows the start-up to ripen to the point of exit. In fact, what actually occurs in such situations is that the entrepreneur sells the idea and enterprise to a bigger company before even enjoying the fruits of its labor. If we wish to translate that into the language of our grandparents, this is its meaning: if you come up with a good idea and you have a successful enterprise, you are not expected to develop and grow your company but rather to sell it to those stronger than you. For example, selling your piece of land that in the past caused wars between countries or between farmers and railway companies is presently accepted in our modern world and is even regarded as the preferable and expected alternative. And who glorifies this alternative if not the global (and mostly not so independent) media?

In newer industries such as the high-tech trade, a similar stagnant situation has evolved in which the giant companies are buying each new enterprise that emerges, thus neutralizing any possible power distribution. As a matter of fact, the Western economy of today has stopped being competitive or innovative in the capitalistic sense and is now in the corporation era. Entrepreneurs are not competing with the old corporations and there old stagnated ways. Instead, start-ups in the initial stages are now usually purchased by those corporations, and the two parties can discuss what, if any, capital investments should be given to nourish the new idea.

Coping with the Advantages

Clearly, the corporate method does not just have drawbacks. It responds to the real and psychological needs of people, or else it could not have survived and flourished. In our world, where the religious, feudal, and national methods have disappointed many people and have not managed to form stable and crisis-free orders (but at times have even caused additional crises), the natural tendency is to seek other methods that may lead to a more calm and stable life. As I have already argued in the section about the international arena, there is a possibility here for comprehensible contradiction regarding the will of the corporations to gain national cover in order to energize workers to create motivation for greater output in competing with other nation's workers.

According to another argument, the entire issue of governance in an international corporation is based on the divide-and-rule method; namely, preventing workers from banding together on social-economic lines by fostering competitiveness with ethnic or religious discriminations. Opposite to this argument, there is an increasing perception that international corporations are diverse groups when it comes to ethnicity or religion and, therefore, do not discriminate among their employees and relate to them equally. Therefore, the thinking goes, this enlightened atmosphere beats the old perceptions, and their disappearance from the world is something to be desired. Indeed, this is a legitimate point, but there are those who may claim that equality among people is not a separate idea per se, but one that exists only to enable development and growth for every human being, regardless of ethnicity, faith, or any other possible difference among people. Even if we assume that the international corporation does indeed encourage a sense of equality, what good does it serve when there is no way to break through the glass ceiling and reach international leadership or the narrow, global layers of leadership?

Due to its size, the corporation is also perceived as more economically stable, and, because it invests in many fields in various countries, there is actually no reason for it to disappear or go bankrupt; it will always have enough to sustain itself and support the existence of its employees. This is an erroneous perception, for as we have already realized, the corporation is not worried about firing its workers and temporarily or permanently leaving one of its international locations. The corporation's decisions are all based on its needs and profits. In fact, it is the very flexibility and stamina that enables the international corporation to withstand some of the global economic crises that causes many to lose their jobs and the source of their dignity. Its economic size and labor importance together with its wide political influence encourages the local régimes and politicians to support the corporation in times of economic need, when public funds are already dwindling.

Through economic observation, it may be said that the international corporation uses its size to leverage the economic relations and commerce among countries and continents. This includes investments and developments that were not executed before due to the size of some small nations, economic target audiences, and internal/external political complexities that are prevalent in the multinational arena. This is all very well to say if we are discussing adherence to the leverage of projects and collection of the industry profits without special cultural or social design or after effects and movement up the career ladder for the working public (abolishment of the glass ceiling). When the impact causes more harm than good, however, a different kind of thinking should be applied.

The Solutions

The answer to greedy capitalism and the power of the corporation is this: return the independence to the individual economical unit. One way to accomplish this is to ensure that most homeowners in the community have energy independence. I can present a few examples: using sun receptor panels to turn energy into accumulated electricity; distilling water with a home purification device; recycling garbage as organic fertilizer in the domestic hothouse; raising livestock on the family's property to eat. When individuals are no longer dependent on electricity and water resources, they can physically survive without contact points with the corporations, which are also the points through which corporations impose their wishes. Thus, such a group of families can strengthen the true communality among them. In the future, the privatization of the space vehicles industry by encouraging young companies to compete with Boeing and the ability to create greenhouse oxygen may enable individuals to develop settlements in space.

The future of humanity depends on its ability to escape the tyranny of the greedy capitalistic elite who control the corporations. The faster individuals regain their potential independence, the greater the possibility to reconstruct, with more agility, the conditions that motivated the settlers to move west to the Great Plains beyond the Appalachians. Such perceptions established the reason for the great cultural, economic, and social development in the United States, a nation that consisted of thousands upon thousands of independent immigrants who had built their lives without any dependence on a political, social, or economic culture beyond the fences of their homesteads.

Such a coping mode must be combined with a return to the gold standard as the leading principle of economic policy. After the gold standard was cancelled in the American economy, a subculture of prosperity evolved based on nothing at all. The financial guarantees were not worth the paper on which they were written. It started as an experiment and ended as a mistake of hysterical and historical dimensions. Since then, People made their fortunes based on wishes backed up with piles of worthless paper. A stable economy with a stable and burgeoning horizon on a super global level requires resources that serve as criteria. Gold is a criterion that does not lie; according to scientists it exists in other worlds, too, and should another tangible criterion be needed, so be it. That criterion must be concrete and durable, and it must be quantifiable and measurable with exact finality in any given moment.

Education is also an excellent device for coping with the repercussions of corporation rule in the long term. It is interesting to note that Judaism, on a small scale, engaged in an informal experiment that pointed at a failed solution for the current situation. During the nineteenth century, following the promises given in the previous century through the French Revolution and then by Napoleon, the European Age of Enlightenment "invaded" European Jewry. Jews were the last to be tempted to join the progress and links of the "corporations" and the elite in those days (national elite and political leading elite). Consequently, many young people broke away from traditional frameworks and started a journey toward broader general education and the promised emancipation. Unfortunately, many European Christians refused to accept the new "citizens of the world" with open arms, and perhaps the young Jews' actual resemblance to the nation in which they lived intensified the fears and inflamed the hatred against them. The reaction of the religious Jewry was an interesting one: it developed the model of the professional student, the eternal, educated *yeshiva* male student, who was supported by the community and placed at the top of its desired scale of values.[5] Gradually, the rabbis turned students who were familiar with the Bible—the intelligent ones, who understood life and the needs of the human being—into men who excelled in the knowledge of the Jewish law but were, in fact, detached from the day-to-day lives of their people.

That *yeshiva* student culture was copied in its entirety in Israel by the ultraorthodox circles and then developed and improved according

---

5 A *yeshiva* is a Jewish religious day school for males only.

to their own basic needs. It provided and educated an audience who listened to the "viewpoints" of those who excelled in their theology studies. Yet, it detached itself from the human's personal flow of actions, which in turn increased the alienation between religious students who adhered to the values of this culture and the secular students who were working for a living with its joy of material creation.

In the light of this historical experiment it is my believe that in a world where information is actually found at our fingertips, the answer does not lie in unidirectional education searching for excellence. To respond to the world of corporate elites, individuals must rely on education for the old and tested values such as love of others; charity; support of the weak; and strengthening community ties and the basic familial unit. During a young person's early years, there is a need to educate him or her about values supported by historical examples that are consistent with these values (the Boston Tea Party, Bunker Hill, the Battle of the Alamo, the Gettysburg Address, and so on). Later on in their studies, students should be given more intricate and profound examples that justify the establishment of these basic values. Simultaneously, students should also learn to take a critical approach to examining and justifying new values that emerge from the public. Finally, there is a need to emphasize the study and analysis of social, economic, political, and historical processes. Knowledge of such analyses will serve students throughout life; there will be no need for informational study and to search for obscure databases after students learn how to use and process the ever-flowing information.

After eight years of study, a graduate should be informed and have values. After twelve years of study, a graduate should have values, be able to think critically, and have basic analytical ability.

Beyond providing students with actual professional information (doctor, geologist, scientist, accountant, and so on), the academic world should offer, free of charge, courses for the gifted who are truly interested in the thinking modes and theories of doctrines. In addition, special pedagogical attention should be paid to all those who turn to the teaching field—both those who choose to become teachers and those who choose to be lecturers in the academia world.

Religion may also act as a springboard for individuals in coping with the world of corporations. There is a need to stay away from the interpretations regarding the connection between material success and spiritual success as a necessity. Fulfillment of faith must, first and foremost, require full control of the basic set of values and then the comprehension of the human psyche, clear perception of intricate systems, and intelligence. Only at the end of the spiritual path is there some value in learning about the know-how. The measure of success in this world does not necessarily point at the financial "God's blessing" of the followers. Yes for material wealth, but only if the person has withstood the criteria of the required values. Values are not less important than material success.

Another important way for individuals to resist the dictations of corporate fashion and culture is to preserve the cultural elite (see the following paragraph) as independent and ensure support by governmental and public funds and institutions. This is necessary to prevent the turning of all culture into part of the corporation's campaign.

The core of cultural elite, which includes literati, poets, dancers, playwrights, film makers, sculptors, painters, and so on, shall forever be preserved through its authentic multifaceted elitism, which supports the freedom of creation as well as different and separate viewpoints. For example, it does not matter if you like Michael Moore, because his movies and lectures provide some balance to the other side's opinion in a public debate. Note that I do not identify with the way Moore explains the picture of the world; nevertheless, his existence, and that of many like him (as a conservative, I do hope they do not share precisely the same outlook), is imperative in order to balance the public's picture of the world as it is spread before us. The very existence of such independent film makers forms cracks in the world view promoted by corporations, which streams through the media they own and into the major boulevard of public consciousness.

The role of the cultural elite is to create counter scenarios and perceptual alternatives to the major flow of thought. Nurturing these elite, in our present condition, may help us regain a more balanced world picture with a mixture of greater community and local characteristics.

On a personal note, I also believe that preservation of family connections and their cultural and social enhancements in all kinds of nuclear or extended families enforces the social texture and makes it difficult for the impact of the corporations to penetrate humanity's last fortress. (Don't we often ask what has happened to daily family meals and why they have vanished from the media?)

On the international level, the corporation should be given a familiar and identifiable place among international organizations in the sense of "see and be warned." International connections and organizations must also be strengthened, especially the ones dealing with international commerce and anti-criminal collaborations such as the Interpol and the international courts for commerce and taxing.

Summary
I wrote this article with apprehension about the fate of the human spirit, wherever it is. Ethnicity or religious and sexual preferences do not change the value of the person or his or her moral structure. The problem is not just that the increasing power of the corporation is dragging the social structure of humanity backward to the period of feudalism (a time when a small, rich minority had most of the wealth and was impenetrable to newcomers from the lower classes, while using some small auxiliary groups, ruling the world of economic and cultural vassals). On top of that, the corporation's dominance negates individual human advancement among the majority of populations and stifles long-range creativity that is opulent with imagination.

As with any competitive structure with an impermeable glass ceiling, the corporation prefers mediocre employees over the bright and different, which may undermine the social order on which the foundations of the corporate world are based. In such a world, which lacks the true essence of morality and in which every person is used as a tool for profit and power, the value of the individual declines whereas the value of marketing fables increases. This is the hour of the matrix. All these selfish ideas are reinforced in young people's brains by the same corporations that will employ them during adolescence and exploit their entrepreneurship entirely when they are mature. Such exploitation will not contribute a thing to these young people, but instead will serve as a platform for additional accumulation of money and power in the hands of the few. That has a political, national, and international impact on our world.

This is no longer the capitalism familiar to us and for the sake of which ideological struggles were held throughout the world during the twentieth century. This is a totally new, dangerous, predatory, and almost unprecedented kind of force that is to capitalism what capitalism was to mercantilism.

Should all the steps indicated at the end of this chapter (and perhaps many others too) be adopted, then we may say that the national political system we have been familiar with for the last few centuries was saved in the very last minute of the game. The value of the moral and normative argument shall rise in the world, and again we may be able to talk about human ideologies, beliefs, and feelings. The race for the next possession will be decelerated, and the human mind will gain some rest. Yet, this is not rest for the sake of idleness but rest in order to actualize the destiny of the human pursuit. If we did touch the stars through the power of our imagination, there is no reason why, with the power of our entrepreneurship and ability to grow, we cannot reach them to expand discoveries and the social and the cultural growth of the human species. No corporation will take us to that place if, on the way toward it, we lose our values and the "we" (meaning "ourselves") turns into something else. Let us venture again toward the Appalachian Mountains and visit what was promised to us by our imagination and love of life. People, come back home.

CHAPTER 2:

FOR MY BROTHERS' AND COMPANIONS' SAKE, I WILL NOW SAY...

(Psalms 122:8)
The Creation of the Inner Jewish Rifts

Indifference and neglect often do much more damage than outright dislike.
—*J. K. Rowling,* **Harry Potter and the Order of the Phoenix**

Introduction
In this essay I shall try to show how one of the major problems in the state of Israel's systems stems from the social absence of a consenting elite that carries with it social rules of the game and communal stability. Excluding many groups of citizens from leading positions in the state harmed the reliability of the founders' class, which was supposed to turn into the foundation of such an elite. The lack that evolved was discerned in everything, and it is one of the major causes for the deterioration of the cohesion and loyalty of Israel's citizens.

About the Issues between the Sons of Isaac and the Sons of Ishmael
In the beginning, the East European (Ashkenazi) pioneers came to the Promised Land trying to create something out of nothing. This something was both individual and national: a new prototype of a

Jew and a new Jewish state. These pioneers chose the example of the local Arabs, glorifying the myth of the noble Arab. The frictions and the hostilities between the two diverse social groups as well as the incoming migration of West European bourgeois Jewry, who were less committed to the ideologies and values, led to the repression of that romantic image. Gradually this romantic reflection was exchanged with the perception of Arabs as tribal people with an inferior and backward culture.

The Hatred of the Centuries-long Exile Status and its Influence on the Jews

During the era of enlightenment, the West European Jews preferred to create a new image of the European Jew without the distresses and deviations of the Diaspora. Consequently, some of the old spiritual leadership, and some of the remaining people leading the Yiddish culture, were slandered and left on the side. Some of the East European Jews followed in their footsteps, accompanied with the first and second Zionist waves.

All at once, the experience based upon the nation and its community's thousands of leadership years was considered to be typical for the Diaspora. Later on, accusations were also leveled at the Diaspora leadership's refusal to confront the gentile land owners, which resulted in the entire community marching into the Nazi gas chambers like sheep to the slaughter. The leaders were accused of this because of their Diaspora blindness. In other, more horrible cases, some leaders were accused of collaborating with the oppressors, and thus the ultimate betrayal of the Jewish people.

The Diaspora model was erased, and the partisans and the leaders of the ghetto rebellions were considered as unique anomalies and not as important parts of the nation's reaction. They were considered the exceptional ones; however, the reaction of the New Hebrew settlement in the country was different. It could be exemplified through the heroic actions of citizens such as Hanna Szenes, to name one example of a great heroine.[6]

During WWII, an entire generation of rabbis and intellectuals was erased in Europe, so anyone who came to Israel (then British Palestine) after the Holocaust could only cling to the nostalgia of the past. But in fact, one had to undertake the new "rules of the game" in the homeland. This meant burying the Diaspora identity with the full deliberate cooperation of the Jews in the land of Israel. This is the ground from which the famous artists such as Dan Ben-Amotz and Ephraim Kishon were evolved.[7]

In addition to that, difficult questions were asked by the Holocaust survivors as well as the local Israelis about how God had allowed the Holocaust to happen. This caused many of the European Jews that came as war refugees to the holy land to leave the realm of religion and abandon the old balance of faith alongside practical life. As a rule, the European Jews distanced themselves from the faith and concentrated instead on building the homeland as well as their new private homes and families. Again, all that was done on the basis of values that negated whatever was related to the Diaspora.

Those Jewish survivors who did not distance themselves from religion chose to shut themselves within their orthodox quarters and diminish their contacts with the world outside the boundaries of their Israeli neighborhoods. A small portion of the religious Jews continued to cling to the Zionist idea, and they wished for unique and separate

---

6 Hanna Szenes was one of thirty-seven Jews from Mandatory Palestine parachuted by the British Army into Yugoslavia during the Second World War to assist in the rescue of Hungarian Jews. Szenes was arrested at the Hungarian border and then imprisoned and tortured, and eventually tried and executed by a firing squad. (Wikipedia, s.v. "Hanna Szenes", last modified May 22, 2015, https://en.wikipedia.org/wiki/Hannah_Szenes)

7 Dan Ben-Amotz was born Moshe Tehilimzeigger, an Israeli radio broadcaster, journalist, playwright and author who was often considered as the most typical "Sabra"—Israeli born. Ephraim Kishon was born Ferenc Hoffmann in Hungary, a famous Israeli author, dramatist, screenwriter and Oscar-nominated film director. He was one of the most widely read contemporary satirists in the world.

definitions of values to be exercised practically, which they achieved, unintentionally, through the victory of the Six-Day War. Among both religious and ultraorthodox immigrants, alternative elites evolved, but they were irrelevant to the rest of the population.

The Sephardic Jews from the Islamic countries who came to Israel following the foundation of the state were mostly ashamed of their origin, which seemed inferior to that of the Western Ashkenazi Jews, and out of inferiority feelings felt a sense of self-denial opposite the Western culture. Some of them were illiterate, some had many children without economic means to bring them up, many did not have professions that could be useful in Israel, and so on. Due to Israel's conflict with the local Arabs, a perception arose that the Arabic culture should be dismissed and was the inferior side in the equation. Thus, it is understandable that many of Sephardic Jews would renounce their forefathers' culture and act as Ashkenazi. The fact that they arrived in the country after its foundations were established and after the ethos and myth of the new Jew, the Sabra, was formed turned them into accomplices to these ideas. Instead of undertaking the position of a bridge between cultures, some of the Jews from Islamic countries turned into the biggest haters and supporters of the anti-Arabic groups in politics as well as in domestic culture. In contrast, anything Western was considered as the object of imitation and esteem.

About the Rejection

Duality evolved among the Jews from Islamic countries (called the Sephardic Jews) about the Ashkenazi establishment, for despite their genuine wish it was impossible for them, figuratively speaking, to "whiten their skin." Because many Ashkenazi Jews were repulsed by the Sephardic Jews Arabic culture and appearance and therefore discriminated against them, they (the Sephardic Jews) had nostalgic emotions about their background. Such nostalgia in their case was not diminished by questions about why the Holocaust took place or the need to create a new Jew through the melting pot. The reasons for that was because many of their Sephardic wise men, their poets and their rabbis were still alive, their leadership and cultural traditions acted as a sanctuary from the lack of acceptance by the Ashkenazi society.

On the side lines, the Israeli Arabs, who were excluded from any kind of impact and felt a growing rejection from their culture, formed individual political frameworks aimed at rehabilitating their cultural and spiritual image. They left the big political parties in which their true impact was never felt.

About the Punishment

When the revolt took place in Wadi Salib (in Haifa),[8] and the leaders of the Black Panthers a decade later saluted it retroactively,[9] the families of the political leadership, as well as all the state's institutions, were marked as being oppressive and discriminatory.

When the political parties Tami and Shas were founded,[10] their political platform called for the restoration of the Sephardic Jewry's past glory, even though many of these Sephardic Jews still bowed before the

---

8 The *Black Panthers* (established in 1971) was an Israeli protest movement of second-generation Jewish immigrants from Middle Eastern countries. They were one of the first organizations in Israel with the mission of working for social justice for the Sephardic Jews. (Wikipedia, s.v. "Black Panthers (Israel)," last modified June 24, 2015, https://en.wikipedia.org/wiki/Black_Panthers_(Israel))

9 On July 10, 1959, several hundred inhabitants in Wadi Salib started the riots. It was claimed the riots were not completely spontaneous, and that a local movement, Union of North-African Immigrants, was involved in planning some of them. The Wadi Salib riots still resonate in Israeli society as a symptom of the social malaise in the early years of the state that led to clashes between Sephardic and Ashkenazi Jews. (Schechter, A. (2012). July 9, 1959: Wadi Salib Riots, www.haaretz.com/Jewish-world.)

10 *Tami* was a Sephardi-dominated political party in Israel during the 1980s. It was led by Aharon Abuhatzira for its entire existence. *Shas* is an ultraorthodox religious political party in Israel. Founded in 1984 under the leadership of Rabbi Ovadia Yosef, a former Israeli Sephardi chief rabbi. It primarily represents the interests of Haredi Sephardic and traditional Sephardic Jews. Originally a small ethnic political group, Shas is currently Israel's seventh largest party in the Knesset. (Wikipedia, s.v.

religious Ashkenazi scholastics (e.g., the children of the Shas leaders were sent to Ashkenazi schools). Still, that call had vigorously beaten the secular-scholastic perception, and, in fact, it delegitimized the secular elite leadership, which was known to have established many, if not all of the state's political, cultural, and educational movements, up to the Supreme Court and the entire justice system.

In its educational system, the Shas party challenged the idea of secular scholastics and especially their theoretical emphases. On the one hand, the Shas party only pointed out the existing gaps between the communities, and on the other hand, it repeatedly and powerfully struck at the features of the elite. From that time onward, and as a political tribute, the un-academically observed qualification for a certified rabbi equaled those of an academic degree, and thus all university studies were perceived as insignificant relative to the study of the Torah Fountain (Jewish theological studies), a study which since then granted the members of the Sephardic religious Jews an academic robe. The slogans of such religious parties included sentence such as "there are no judges in Jerusalem."[11] Their slogans recalled the sayings of the Orthodox Ashkenazi rabbis, calling the nonpious public "rabbit eaters" [12] and ordering their own flock that "one must not mix the blood of those who eat pigs with pure Jewish blood, not even in order to save a life."

At the same time, the Israeli Arabs used the events of Land Day and those events in October 2000 to separate themselves from the state and estrange themselves from their former political existence and turn toward a more relevant and obviously competitive ethos.[13]

"Shas," last modified September 6, 2015, and Wikipedia, s.v. "Tami," last modified July 4, 2015, https://en.wikipedia.org/wiki/Tami)

11 Contrary to a famous saying by Prime Minister Begin.

12 A famous accusation by Rabbi Shach about Kibbutz members.

13 The October 2000 events were a series of protests in Arab villages in northern Israel that turned violent, escalating into rioting by Israeli Arabs. This led to counter-rioting by Israeli Jews, clashes with the Israel police, and ended in the deaths of thirteen Arab demonstrators. The Or Commission was established to investigate the police response to the rioting. Land Day on March 30 is an annual day of commemoration

The Shameful Result

The final result of all the processes described above was the Israeli public's loss of trust in the leadership of the elite, which was considered biased toward the Ashkenazi/European part of Israeli society. It did not leave room for the presentation of alternatives that could help to keep carrying the torch between the different sectors of Israeli society.

During the "melting pot revolution," Israel lost its European-Jewish traditional values, and a few decades later, during the "struggle in the squares" between the election years of 1977–1981, Israel lost its Western secular values. At the same time, the general Israeli public felt profound and increasing aversion to Western culture, whereas the traditional Jews who left the religious circles (mostly Sephardic but also the right wing revisionists) perceived the Jewish religion as the antidote for the past and as a millstone before a glorified future. Contrary to the more religious Jews, for the Ashkenazi secular Jews, who based their theories on liberal or Marxist definitions, religion was perceived as poison. On top of that, the self-denial of the Sephardic spiritual leadership opposite the Ashkenazi one was not overlooked by many of the Sephardic followers. Many of them missed the "Wise Men" style of their forefathers.

At the same time, the bloody events with the Arab populations cemented the loss of basic trust in the social elite among one-fifth of the total Israeli population, for they never had representation within the elite.

Thus, it may be deduced that Israel is a country without a social, consolidated, and consensual elite leadership. And because of this, most citizens are not inculcated in the "rules of the game" or in how boundaries

---

for Palestinians of the events of that date in 1976. In response to the Israeli government's announcement of a plan to expropriate thousands of acres of land for security and settlement purposes, a general strike and marches were organized in Arab towns from the Galilee to the Negev. In the ensuing confrontations with the Israeli army and police, six Arab citizens were killed, about one hundred were wounded, and hundreds of others arrested. (Wikipedia, s.v. "October 2000 events," last modified July 7, 2015, https://en.wikipedia.org/wiki/October_2000_events and Wikipedia, s.v. "Land Day," last modified April 15, 2015, https://en.wikipedia.org/wiki/Land_Day)

between classes or indeed ways of crossing them are supposed to work. It seems as though "any rooster can be a king," and that "the fool makes noise and projects himself more than the wise one."[14]

As seen from this perspective, when the October War oversights became public, the crisis of trust toward the old leadership was already there to exploit.

Violence and Corruption

The final section above introduced a situation in which there are no clear rules or laws of the game but in which there are plenty of social tensions and splits that gnaw into the rule of the law and order on the streets. If we add to that the processes of greedy capitalism, which are promoted by the international corporations the kind that Israel is bound to for obvious reasons, then it seems as though the decline of social values and the phenomenon of "looking after my own interests" encourage the loss of group responsibility and the decomposition of social solidarity. All of these act as catalysts for the internal social violence, which can lead people to murder others merely for using different expressions.

Opposite such deterioration, there is no longer any elite, for it has already been eradicated twice by its own people—once in its Diaspora form and again in its secular Ashkenazi form. Therefore, it seems as though there are no frameworks or consensual impediments (e.g., social conventions) to stop the deterioration. The education system no longer handles social education for values as a main an consistent issue but educates students for individual achievements and success in the corporate world. The media world is also declining and is controlled by a small percentage of the upper class that has adopted the new corporate values. Simultaneously, the world of the Torah, and the spiritual leadership (mainly the Ashkenazi, but also the Sephardic) who relied on past greatness and who lost the connection with it, sank into degeneration

---

14 Paraphrase of famous proverbs from the Babylonian Talmud.

of studying and discussing obscure passages of Jewish religious law and lost much of their relevance for the present generation. This fact was not overlooked by some of the secular and traditional leaders. Hence the presentation of grotesque images in public humor, such as Rabbi Nathanel or Babba Bubba,[15] which symbolize exclusion and odious behavior of spiritual leaders (both Ashkenazi and Sephardic). Once again, as almost as in the dark days of the holocaust, regarding the jewish spiritual and leadership aspect, there is no figure who can bridge the gap between the spiritual needs of the people and lack of leadership.

Like other institutions of order and executive authority, and as part of coping with the challenges of the market culture, the police and other law enforcement authorities are forced to use violence, if only to survive on the streets, and they too no longer implement the law verbatim. The entire law enforcement system tends toward the whirl of corruption and brutal behavior, with many employees lacking human or social conscience. Within this context, there are higher percentages of convictions that are based on false confessions attained deceitfully. There is torture of detainees in detention houses and prisons and concealment of detentions. The use of de facto warrants is perpetually growing to negate liberty; so too is the use of evidence concealment or obscurity when suspects are killed by the security forces. The same attitude is used by the executive authority as well.

As one may guess, the Israeli parliament with the encouragement of elements in its right benches and full support of the religious parties made sure that the wings of the Supreme Court were clipped by offering legislation that is immune to the scrutiny of the Supreme Court; due to fear and helplessness, the judiciary agrees with what is happening. The legislative authority is increasingly corrupted by ignorant and violent representatives, as well as by men of means and other utilitarian elements operating through intermediaries to cover up the common politician's financial need to expedite personal aims.

---

15 Both satirical figures of rabbis in Israeli prime-time TV and Internet shows.

The administrative class has already been replaced by key people in the parties, the representatives of the financing families, and, at times, the crime families. As a result, the executive authority is also afflicted by interested parties and dominance.

The army, the General Security Services, and the Mossad intelligence community are all following in the footsteps of the police; some precede it and some follow it, but the stench of corruption and cover-ups increases in quantity and level as time goes by. Apparently, these leave no room for particularly wide margins of error concerning the self-evident conclusion.

In order for a change to take place the ideological, moonstruck people and the extremists join forces in the political and civic field, fully believing in the righteousness of their path, and willing to sacrifice themselves and others in order to actualize their dreams. This is the point where the prologue ends and the calamity begins.

The Countermeasures before That Day Comes
To begin with, there is a need to make decisions about the elite and its enforcement policies, as well as the intensification of the general rules of the game of social class and the modes of social diffusion and mobility. By definition, the elite shall include members from the spiritual area, scholars, and soldiers who come from all layers of society, all citizens of the Israeli state. The existence of the elite requires the consent of all those in it to operate under the same flag and agreed-upon national symbols. Without such mutual consent for camaraderie among them, they will be "eaten alive." All those who do not conform may lose their canonical positions (though not necessarily the alternative ones) at the top of society because of the need for future educational example to all citizens.

Despite all that, the elite must necessarily represent all the streams, communities, religions, and social groups of interest in the state. In addition, once general theoretical education is enhanced, more emphasis must be placed on teaching group social values, and community members must ensure these values are adhered to. Social punishment for all those who deviate from these rules must be toughened. Moreover, professional journalism must be protected from the domination of corporations and tycoons; this may be achieved when journalists are encouraged to own the media in which they work, and thus prevent such domination.

The rule of the law must be strengthened and punishment enforced in all cases of declared antisocial behavior: street hooliganism, domestic violence, neighborhood violence, hit-and-run accidents and abstaining help when it is needed, embezzlement, betrayal of public trust, corruption, and so on

Social sensitivity should be placed above any kind of personal achievement. There must be care for the weak, honor for one's parents, insistence on the rights of children, and support for minority rights. All these fall within the rules of the game and with the total concurrence of the elite.

Last, but not necessarily a point that everyone will agree upon, there is the necessity to form connections within the framework of the elite between the competing spiritual leadership and the people. Diversity in the local spiritual leadership will energize religious leaders to shape and amend the path to faith while facing the needs of the believer. In parallel, and even if only temporarily due to the given situation, equally valuable channels should be formed that require moral and legal tolerance of lifestyles in which religion plays no part, such as secularism, atheism and so on.

A Word before Signing Off

I do not have a private radar system that can reveal to me what the future holds for the Israeli inhabitants. My predictive ability is based on my understanding of the present. growing a new consensual Elite is far away from any present understanding I might have.

CHAPTER 3

THE HIDDEN TRAP OF SAMSON'S OPTION

The Unforeseen Inner Effect of Having a Doomsday Weapon

To summarize: it is a well-known fact that those people who most want to rule people are, ipso facto, those least suited to do it.
To summarize the summary: anyone who is capable of getting themselves made President should on no account be allowed to do the job.
—**Douglas Adams**, **The Restaurant at the End of the Universe**

Clarification

This chapter is based on the assumption of the State of Israel's nuclear capability, supported by publications in foreign sources. The title alludes to *The Samson Option: Israel's Nuclear Arsenal and American Foreign Policy*, a 1991 book by Seymour Hersh. It details the history of Israel's supposed nuclear weapons program and its effects on Israel-American relations. The Samson Option refers to the nuclear strategy whereby Israel would launch a massive nuclear retaliatory strike if the state itself was being over-run, just as the biblical figure Samson is said to have pushed apart the pillars of a Philistine temple, bringing down the roof and killing himself and thousands of Philistines who had gathered to see him humiliated.

Introduction

Recent decades have demonstrated a paradox in the state of Israel that, in my opinion, has influenced the economic and political leadership and consequently, the entire population. Samson's Option, which is the Israeli atom option, grants the national leadership great power and ensures the survival of the state in the face of external dangers that threaten Israel's existence. My argument is that although this strengthens the actual survival and existence of the state, it nevertheless weakens the government's perception of inner threats and the governance of its citizens. Because of Israel's nuclear capability—and especially its second-strike capability—its leaders consider the situation as one where there is only a minute essential risk from external enemies. Thus, if there is a Middle East crisis, there is still enough political time, as well as real time, to solve it and eventually finalizing the Israeli move. In contrast to external threats, to which one must eventually respond swiftly and precisely, when social or economic crises concerning the state's citizens are at stake, there is even less need to hurry. Moreover, in the eyes of the ruling class, there may be a desire to delay reaction or use tactics such as humiliating the spokesmen instead of attacking the arguments in order to reject solutions required by the representatives of the various complainants.

This approach relies on the social-political structure in which the rich are close to the people in authority because the former provide economic support to the latter during local and national election campaigns. The government's representatives reward the business leadership through legislation and budgets.

The state's proven ability to cope with the Wadi Salib events,[16] Land Day, the Black Panthers, the October 2000 events, and the social protests of 2011 demonstrates how ineffective the public is when it protests on a social-economic basis that strengthens and reinforces the government's continued behavior. It is the vanity of the strong to implicate from one case to another. Yes, so far Israel is strong confronting its external enemies, but that doesn't indicate a thing about its leadership in-

---

16 The Wadi Salib riots were a series of street demonstrations and acts of vandalism in the Wadi Salib neighborhood of Haifa, Israel, in 1959, sparked by charges of ethnic discrimination by Ashkenazi Jews against Sephardic Jews. (Wikipedia, s.v. "Wadi Salib riots," last modified May 3, 2015, https://en.wikipedia.org/wiki/Wadi_Salib_riots)

ternal strength against underpaid workers or mistreated citizens. These events, all of which are socioeconomically driven at root, are perceived as though they were absorbed by the body of the state without hurting its backbone. However, all of this is only ostensibly so. The perceived moral and social repercussions of such behavior (although these are not revealed to the economic or political leaders during the emotional outbreaks of the protests) gnaw at the foundations of society—at its cohesion, patriotic strength, its acceptance of the burden of government (law and order), and many other relevant points.

The Public's Protest Behaviors

It is well known that the Israeli public is essentially conservative; however, it is also due to the loyalty of the majority and its justified fears of social disorder and how that might threaten the existence of the state that it avoids shock and redundant provocations against the establishment. The perception is one of "don't rock the boat" to keep us from being flooded by the hostile sea surrounding our borders. This existential fear weakens the public's ability to react; in most situations, Israelis simply choose to adapt and come to terms with situations, rather than resort to protest or violence.

The prevailing perception is that one must not confront the government, not only due to conservatism or loyalty but also due to the price paid by the protesting minorities in all the street wars that have taken place so far. After all, no one wishes to be called a "follower of Rabbi Uzi Meshulam."[17]

One way or another, the police always have the upper hand, and the victims' families can lose all they have in an instant. In addition, there is an embedded fear of the long arm of the state in the form of security services. One reason is that examinations of protestors' security

---

17   Uzi Meshulam (October 30, 1952 to June 21, 2013) was a rabbi from Yehud. In 1994 he was the leader of a radical group of Yemenite Jews who violently resisted Israeli law enforcement authorities. (Wikipedia, s.v. "Uzi Meshulam," last modified February 12, 2015, https://en.wikipedia.org/wiki/Uzi_Meshulam)

backgrounds may prevent family members from making progress in their careers. This can occur whether the person is marked as a social activist or is injured in riots. As a result, Israelis who do participate in demonstrations are verbally brave but rarely take concrete action. They need the feeling of support provided by the social net to fight for them even following police arrest, like the mutual support of the ultraorthodox extremists or of the settlers in Judea and Samaria. In these two social sectors, it is possible to see that a social network enables street demonstrations and moderate resistance to the police. This is valid as long as the social network, which handles the issue, actually manages to reduce the detention and punishment of those caught in action. Of course, those who are taken prison are escorted by members of their community and gain political support that is usually all-encompassing, until amnesty is achieved.[18] Thus, the interrogation conditions are also open to public scrutiny.

It should be noted that the security net of ultra-orthodox society is wider because it does not acknowledge the authority of the state as the supreme authority. For them, any subject that is presented by their rabbis as deviating from *Da'at Torah* (Torah opinion) is a legitimate target for protest on the streets.[19] That is why the required support network is big and, indeed, does cover many situations.

In contrast, among the national religious sector, there is no net for demonstrations, only for issues relating to the settlements and the boundaries of the state of Israel. Not all other issues are covered by any communal protection net. Hence, young National Religious people who are arrested by the police during a demonstration about economic or social issues do not get particular support from their community.

---

18 Except for one famous example: Yigal Amir (born May 23, 1970), the murderer of Israeli Prime Minister Yitzhak Rabin.

19 The Pentateuch Da'at Torah means the way of the day-to-day life as structured by the scriptures and rabbis to their traditional congregations (the whole of orthodox Rabbinic teaching).

In comparison to the examples presented so far, Israeli Arabs are most apprehensive about collision with the security authorities. If an individual is marked by the security authorities, it may lead to the family or the entire tribe being marked, which in turn causes delays and problems for travelers when leaving the country, especially on pilgrimages to Mecca, but also on visits to relatives in neighboring countries.

Despite the rise of the Islamic movements among Israeli Arabs, they still prefer to avoid participation in general public protests as much as possible. As a result, such protests remain inside the Arab villages and towns, especially when they concern sector-related issues. In such cases, geographical peripheral policing was gained following past experience of clashes between the local population and police units. Prior to that understanding, those who demonstrated in the streets about the police's methods and restrictions were victimized. At present, it is clear that when there is a demonstration in an Arab village or town, the police prevent entrance of external visitors and restrict themselves to peripheral protection, without entering or rubbing shoulders with the demonstrators. In cases where the security forces have breached regulations, there is a lobby of Arab Knesset members who unite with one of the leftist parties to pressure the government. Such pressure may lead to investigative committees and may also improve the detention or imprisonment conditions of those arrested and ensure supervision of interrogation conditions.

Whereas Arabs, extremist ultraorthodox, and National Religious groups exploit their right to demonstrate according to their own special "scale of values" and with relatively little concern for their individual fates, secular Israelis are devoid of defenses and have ample fears (some of which are justified); therefore, they rarely use these means.

Secular Israeli Jews are caught by the horns of this dilemma: on the one hand, they have no social instruments to support them should they participate in street demonstrations. They are afraid that if they are arrested, no one but their close family will look after them. On the other hand, they do not side with the zero-sum game in which the security risk may cause the loss of the state. As a result, many secular Israelis disassociate themselves from acting out and from protesting against actual danger for any existing regime whatsoever.

The Business Leadership's Mode of Reaction

Regarding economic leadership, as long as the reason for taking to the streets or for undermining public order is not socioeconomic, the upper social class and its representatives are reluctant to display their influence so as not to be labeled as supportive of any particular topic. However, if the said issue has an impact on their profits, position or power in the social hierarchy, they immediately use their government connections to make demands and pressure them, so that only minimal damage, if any, may affect their profits and power.

The members of this limited group play for time through the justified assumption that eroding time lowers the economic price at the end of the road. This is the wisdom of negotiation with representatives of employees during business or plant crises.

The time spent during social crises allows the political leadership to be maneuvered to solutions that would place only minimal limits on the small group of Israeli tycoons and representatives of international companies. In contrast, taking action to solve immediate distress or problems suggested by the citizens is less relevant.

This is all very well during a small-scale demonstration, but when the demonstration reaches national dimensions, lost time may be added to the cognitive dissonance of the leadership. Hence, the process may be stretched out for a long time while pressure on the ground becomes unbearable.

The Political Leadership and Its Mode of Reaction

As far as the political leadership is concerned, knowing the protest patterns of the Israeli public, particularly the secular portion of it, is a real asset that can be used any time protests undermine the leadership's methods and seem to hurt the private interests of those holding the reins. A few randomly released statements about the situation at the border or about war movements among our enemies suffice to publicly deter any loyal citizen from expressing his or her emotions in a way that may harm public order or the government. Here, in my opinion, is another important factor that distorts the ruling political class's perceptions. The Israeli leadership is certain that nuclear weapons, and mainly the second-strike capability, serve as a clear determent against our neighbors and enemies; that its presence will continue to prevent them from intervening. So solid is the belief of the Israeli leadership in the nuclear determent that in their thoughts even if there are socially based riots all over Israel, or a massive wave of outgoing immigration that empties the country of its human resources, nothing severe will happen to the country and its leadership. All this is based on the understanding that the Arab countries that are perceived as the eminent threat to the state of Israel, know that there will be no shortage of hands to press the button in time of need, even in the midst of a revolution. One does not need many fingers in order to press the button or a particular level of education to maintain systems that were in the forefront of global technology until the crisis erupted.

Hence, the leadership's perception is that fundamental problems can only occur externally, and there is still much time to solve the internal crisis, either by ignoring it or through various levels of response through calculation of governmental and personal interests. As far as the time element is concerned, this perception is in complete contrast to the one held by the main segment of the Israeli public who are fearful about rocking the Israeli boat.

Of course, such perception of time by the political leadership is erroneous, because beyond a certain point, the social reaction of the entire public will emerge in the form of violent upheaval or in the form of quiet resistance, but the only true certainty is that the reaction will indeed take place.

I compare this to two hands, palms positioned in front of each other with fingertips touching. If we push one palm against the other, just as circumstances push the public into a state of crisis, we will see that after a while (the reference point that we shall call the last minute), the wrinkles in the skin of the palm that is pushed back are widened. These wrinkles may be compared to the social gaps and cracks that, a moment before the back blow, are starting to be visible again and at times even bleed. Ashkenazi versus Sephardic, secular versus religious, Jews versus non-Jews, rich versus poor—all these are social cracks that, after circumstances cause pressure to begin, expand outwardly and become visible. In our model, from a certain moment onward (we could call it by the way of metaphor "the end of injury time"), the palm that was stretched back can no longer move forward in a slow fashion. For the sake of analogy, the spring was overstretched and through gradually increasing powers, it is aimed at recoiling. When the political and economic leadership is found on the side of circumstance that is causing the stretching of the palm (inside or by leading the other, pushing palm), the recoil will hit hard just like a spring that is suddenly released.

Political leaders may erroneously think that in such cases, time is on their side, but in fact, beyond the specific point of no return, the restrained rage of the masses demands its pound of flesh, and the actions of the leadership no longer have any impact. For me, as a conservative, from a certain point onward, time is part of the problem and is not a basis for solutions.

Contra indications

The mere knowledge of the time obstacle and its acknowledgment together with the understanding that eminent threats can come from the inside as well as from the outside, are contraindicative and enable leaders to examine the state of their internal affairs congruently with the measure of existing social fermentation and take timely action to prevent damage to the frameworks of the rule and the state.

Summary

The tragedy of the present situation is that given Israel's geographical location and the striking contrasts between its world views and those of its neighbors, it cannot be rid of nuclear weapons. Losing the deterrent of the second strike may cause the country's demise through a series of attacks that will not end until it is actually overpowered.

However, as I claim in this chapter, the actual existence of the atomic deterrent option, reinforced with the knowledge of Israeli protest patterns, blinds political and business leaders to what is happening internally and prevents them from seeing the true severity of the social and economic extremities. In such case, a serious internal crisis may turn into a danger that is not less severe, and it may take the form of violence without proper response from the leadership due to false perception of time. Such a crisis may shuffle the cards and badly harm the government and the state's existence.

CHAPTER 4

JEWISH STATE AND THE ARAB-ISRAELI CONFLICT

Nationalism on Shaky Ground

*M**y concern is not whether God is on our side; my greatest concern is to be on God's side, for God is always right.***
—Abraham Lincoln

My Perspective as Participant in this Conflict
In my youth, a central issue that we discussed at youth movements and in social studies classes was whether we consider ourselves Jews and then Israelis, or vice versa. Years later, as a young student living on Kibbutz Kiryat Anavim, while attending a program that provided food and board in return for work, I met Old Man Dov. Dov was a Holocaust survivor who had come to the kibbutz as an elderly man. By the 1990s he was almost a hundred years old. The life stories of Dov and his wife had a strong impact on me, but one thing in particular remained etched in my mind: the name he adopted in Israel, Yehudi Ben-Amo (a Jew, a son of his nation). My values are those of a progressive conservative, and I believe in God. Since my youth, and especially since meeting Old Man Dov, I have considered myself a human being first, a Jew, an Israeli, and a Zionist, respectively. There are two sayings I particularly connected with as a young man. The one that contributed to my conservatism was that "new meat is eaten with old forks"

(Bertolt Brecht). The one that helped me to form my concept of humanity and of what it takes to be a human being was "in a place where there are no men, strive to be a man" (Pirkei Avot 2:5). These had a strong impact on my Zionist outlook. If this, too, needs to be defined, I could summarize by saying I am a pragmatic Zionist, born to parents who followed two parties: the Avoda party (Israeli Labor Party) and the Beitar party.[20]

Introduction

This chapter analyzes factions of the Jewish people living in Israel that currently constitute the majority of Israel's population. Toward the end of the chapter, I mention Israel's Arab civilian population and some of their perspective on the issues. Let me remind the wise reader that this book is not intended to be a balanced historical record of the Arab-Israeli conflict. The only reason I write about the conflict is to show the effects it had according to my point of view on Israel's social decline.

The Zionist movement was a relatively late phenomenon of a broad national awakening that occurred in nineteenth-century Europe. Folk

---

20 Labor Zionism is the primary stream of the Zionist movement's left wing. For many years, it was the most influential party among Zionists and Zionist organizational structure. It considered itself to be the Zionist sector of the historic Jewish labor movements of Eastern and Central Europe, eventually developing local units in most countries with sizeable Jewish populations. Unlike adherents of political Zionism, founded by Theodor Herzl and advocated by Chaim Weizmann, Labor Zionists did not believe that a Jewish state would be created simply by appealing to the international community or to powerful nations such as Britain, Germany, or the Ottoman Empire. Rather, Labor Zionists believed that a Jewish state could be created only through the efforts of the Jewish working class settling in Palestine and establishing a state through the formation of a progressive Jewish society with rural kibbutzim, moshavim, and an urban Jewish proletariat. (Wikipedia, s.v. "Labor Zionism," last modified July 14, 2015, https://en.wikipedia.org/wiki/Labor_Zionism) The Betar movement is a revisionist Zionist youth movement founded in 1923 in Riga, Latvia, by Vladimir (Ze'ev) Jabotinsky. branches sprang up across Europe, even during World War II. After the war and during the settlement of what became Israel, Betar was traditionally linked to the original Herut and then Likud political parties of Jewish pioneers. (Wikipedia, s.v. "Betar," last modified June 22, 2015, https://en.wikipedia.org/wiki/Betar)

movements sought national freedom and self-definition within their re-gions, contrary to old-school imperialistic countries (Austria-Hungary, Great Russia), as part of a dream of greatness that stemmed from estab-lishing a national identity. This vision was shared even by neighboring national fractions originating from earlier tribal divisions (as seen in the case of modern Germany and Italy). By definition, these movements are secular because the nation claims ownership of geographical land with joint ripples of myth and ethos. The source of sovereignty is the people and not God, as opposed to earlier monarchy or emperor model. Since the establishment of the nation-state, we have citizens of the same nationality whose mere presence justifies sovereignty.

At this point, it is important to address the confusion that exists in Israel regarding this issue: academically in the boundaries of the state of Israel it should always be Jewish peoplehood and not Jewish nationality; Palestinian peoplehood and not its (pending) nationality. Nationality is defined as Israeli for all citizens of the state. The power of Israeli nationality is measured by its ability to establish myths and ethos held by its entire people regardless of religion, race, or gender.

The state of Israel was founded on the ideas of Zionism's centrist movements, which primarily maintained national and ethnical prag-matism. This unique ideological creation has always faced difficulties establishing and containing myths and ethos shared by all the people of the land, surprisingly also among the Jewish people themselves.

In the next few paragraphs, I intend to present a historical perspec-tive of the current attitude of various populations, primarily that of the various groups among the Jewish people, in their perception of the state and its essence.

The Haredi (Ultraorthodox) Population

Israel's Haredi population is currently experiencing one of the lowest so-cial points of its history in the state of Israel. As a rule, due to a very nar-row-sighted leadership, grown individual Haredis lack the knowledge required to lead a modern, developed country in the twenty-first century. As individuals, they lack general education regarding Israeli culture, including high-tech entrepreneurship, science and industry studies. A lack of scientific and technological capability is accompanied by lack of understanding about the work market needs and of basic local professional demands. This leaves many of them far behind Israel's primary workforce.

As a result of their belief system—which leaves no space for shades of gray—Israeli Haredis are generally highly dogmatic in their outlook and are, therefore, unable to compromise with public situations by taking into account other population segments' beliefs or with the physical proximity of separate worlds of content and culture. Fears about standing out and/or of being ostracized by their own people impair the Haredis' ability to lead lives that differ even slightly from the safe, familiar lives of their Haredi neighbors.

In addition, there is a leadership crisis among Israel's Haredi population due to cultural and social decline. This decline stems from the integration of the yeshiva learning system with the system of governmental long-lasting livelihood support, preventing people from stepping into the outside world. This system of financial support, by over defending its participants, bypasses cultural and moral obstacles, which are usually the catalysts for new religious rules and perceptions that lead in their own point in time to the formation of new conceptual and legal pious establishments. This unique Israeli system has created a sense of mediocrity for yeshiva graduates who learn how to recite Halakha (Jewish religious law) passed down by their ancestors but can't proclaim an old text book case to be the basis for a much-needed modern ruling. It seems like we might have in Israel a new generation of yeshiva graduates who lack the courage or leverage to utilize their own minds to take a stand and innovate within the boundaries of the Halakha. To make matters worse, the yeshivas are widely accessible and heavily subsidized, which has encouraged the formation of a wide younger generation that, intellectually speaking, does not try very hard. These students are not particularly interested in learning and rather use the yeshivas as a comfortable hiding place while they receive governmental Monetary support. The existence of this growing population does not inspire excellence. Quite the opposite: it encourages mediocrity yet again. Down the line, as so many people abide by mediocre interpretations of Jewish law, lacking ingenuity, there is a great deal of pressure on those who do excel, even as far as instilling fear in them not to introduce new concepts or to take the lead.

This means that even within the limitations of Halakha, yeshiva students in Israel do not constitute a driving worldwide force in Jewish studies. As a result leadership is gradually granted to Jews in the United States, who have taken a different approach. In the United States, there are no government-subsidized ghettos or cultural blocks for the Haredi population. Instead, there is an emphasis on integration into the workplace and a much-needed blending of Halakha with twenty-first-century challenges.

In Israel, there wasn't (and still isn't) nationalized core education in yeshivas (i.e., history of the Jewish people, civics, English, sciences, and so on) and because the Haredi population is spiritually close to the national religious Jews, a link exists between the two religious movements regarding assessing statehood. This was based on the Haredi only de facto recognition of the state of Israel, as well as ignorance and a lack of acceptance of state introduced tools for core education. When facing nationalism as a political agenda, many of the Haredi accept the rulings of National Religious Jews as the better of two evils, especially when considering the alternative of the secular Jews.

Furthermore, and as a final example showing the depth of the denial of parts of reality in the Haredi society, every Haredi can cite that in their studying, they deal entirely with the world of the written Halakha word; therefore, the world outside of this written word is considered invalid.

In the times of the Gedolim (the great rabbinical scholars), from Avrohom Yeshaya Karelitz to Elazar Shach, who both lived in Israel, such rabbis demonstrated an ability to present an outlook encompassing areas not included by Halakha.[21] These rabbis' congregation members accepted this outlook with their customary obedience; however, currently there is increasing demand on behalf of Haredis for the Halakha's perspective on their daily modern lives. This stems primarily from the fact that many Gedolim are living nowadays in the Diaspora. This existing geographical distance that is coupled also with a cultural gap naturally prevents a comprehensive approach to the needs of Haredis that live Israel for Halakha interpretations regarding the individual and the nation-state that purports to be a Jewish state.

The Israeli Haredi population, therefore, is in the most spiritually vulnerable condition ever, suffering the over fortified walls of Halakha without any conjunction with the Hashkufeh, which covers territory that Halakha does not.[22] It also lacks the intellectual, modern tools necessary for the analysis and understanding of the Jewish nation's state and assessing its moral soul.

The Secular Population
During the early years of prestatehood, as befitting the Zionist dream of creating a new country and a new type of Jew, the secular Jew has lost touch with tradition. This social and cultural innovation apparently required cutting ties with the conventions of Diaspora Jews, leading to the loss of hundreds of years of tradition, characterizing the people's rich experiences outside of their own land. The Israeli pioneer embodied the

---

21 Avrohom Yeshaya Karelitz (1878–1953), known by the name of his magnum opus *Chazon Ish*, was a Belarusian-born Orthodox rabbi who later became one of the leaders of Haredi Judaism in Israel. (Wikipedia, s.v. "Avrohom Yeshaya Karelitz," last modified June 12, 2015, https://en.wikipedia.org/wiki/Avrohom_Yeshaya_Karelitz) Elazar Menachem Man Shach, also spelled Eliezer Schach or Elazar Shach (1899–2001) was a leading Lithuanian-born and -educated Haredi rabbi in Bnei Brak, Israel. (Wikipedia, s.v. "Elazar Shach," last modified July 5, 2015, https://en.wikipedia.org/wiki/Elazar_Shach)

22 Hashkufeh: an ideology of values based on the teachings of an influential Haredi rabbi, obligating its body of followers.

value of love for working the land, preferring this over bourgeois work due to the need for redemption of land and man. However, these pioneers did not seek redemption through the Jewish religion; instead they strove for a strictly secular creation, alienating religion and requiring detachment from the ethos and the culture of the Diaspora. Gradually, the name of this new creation as the "religion of work" took root. A different approach as taken by pioneers such as A. D. Gordon, who explicitly combined the recognition of Jewish tradition with this new creation, became rare in the pre-Israeli landscape.[23]

With the establishment of the state, the secular population gradually lost its Zionist outlook, if only because the revolution as a philosophy was perceived as a success and people went their separate ways after finishing their group task. The individual lost the Zionist drive and became open to an altered value system that may accompany capital and property. As people looked to the West, the taking on of a consumer culture became more desirable. However, the return of those former pioneers to an individual perspective was missing one aspect from the old Diaspora that also existed in one way or another in Western countries: community as a social value and as a network for protecting the individual.

The Yom Kippur War constituted a critical blow to Zionist secular nationalism; up until that point, Israel was led by central factions of the secularist sect. On the one hand, it has been proven that the state withstood the fateful test. For all those who did not comprehend beforehand, the establishment of a stable state, Zionism's core mission, was now proven to be complete. On the other hand, during a time of trial and tribulation, all established secular national symbols were a disappointment. To a certain degree, the Israeli Defense Forces (IDF) was a disappointment.

---

23 Aaron David Gordon (1856–1922), more commonly known as A. D. Gordon, was a Zionist ideologue and the spiritual force behind practical Zionism and Labor Zionism. He founded Hapoel Hatzair, a movement that set the tone for the Zionist movement for many years to come. Influenced by Leo Tolstoy and others, he is said to have formed, in effect, a religion of labor. (Wikipedia, s.v. "A. D. Gordon," last modified May 23, 2015, https://en.wikipedia.org/wiki/A._D._Gordon)

The military high command and political elite were a disappointment. There was an understanding that the war did not end in defeat mainly because of the heroism of individuals and the assistance of the American superpower, and not because of a special leadership effort. One has to remember that we are talking about the same state that in all the pompousness following the Six Days War, only six years before, had no place for comforting or caring for those suffering from its aftershock. Not because they didn't exist, but because their behavior was not considered to be the true Israeli representation of winner's honor and grace.

All of these factors acted as a driving force behind some secularists' cynicism toward the state and its values. Many went their separate ways, even at the public's expense. Others chose to search abroad with others like them for comfort and togetherness, nurturing the widening gap in their souls during time of war, while others searched for cults and eastern mysticism, or reinforced their Judaism and ultimately became "newly born" Jews.

Within the secular perspective after leaving Zionism, there is a troubling vacuum of community values where everything leans toward self-achievement and revolves around profit and personal accomplishment. This vacuum was also felt by Sephardic Jews (Jews descended from local Jewish communities in the Middle East) who had immigrated to Israel during the nineteen fifties.

Traditional Immigrants from Arab Countries
From day one, the view of the Ashkenazi (Jews descended from local Jewish communities in European societies) about the creation of a new prototype of a Jewish person as "first in line" clashed with values of tradition, community, and close human relations held by immigrants from Arab countries. The rejection the Sephardi immigrants experienced by Ashkenazi Jews meant that the culture they brought with them would be kept underground, waiting for the right time to be exposed. The crisis of the Yom Kippur War allowed Sephardic Jews a first chance to see that they

were able to bring about changes in Israel, and that they could be freed from conceptual and cultural coercion by the Ashkenazi cultural dream. This feeling, along with the fumes of the Wadi Salib riots and the Black Panthers sent Sephardic Jews on a voyage that would change values and perceptions in a country that was previously run according to Western values. This is the population that brought about the Israeli ethnic revolution.

Along with this awakening came a murky cloud of old-fashioned views from the Sephardic Jews' home countries. Nationalism was a movement with ideas that developed in Europe and was imported by local Eastern intellectuals and was late to meet the cultures of North Africa and the Middle East. In most of their countries of origin, Sephardic Jews did not experience a comprehensive nationalist movement encompassing all populations with a myth and ethos accepted by all citizens. The Muslim world's multitude of Islamic religious outlooks, that combine state and religion together, ruled out European nationalism, and this approach governed extensive sections of the popular and public landscape in those countries. It is evident that the Sephardic traditionalists' relationship with the nation-state of Israel reflected the general outlook from their countries of origin and was based upon the biblical vision of resurrecting the people of Israel. The idea of a nation as a sovereign entity by and for all of its citizens was and still is completely foreign to many of them. Even at present, many of the Sephardic Jews believe that the state is attributed to a divine biblical promise to members of the Jewish people (with or without the Ashkenazi, now considered by some extremist Sephardic Jews to be descendants of the Khazars, thereby distinguishing them from the indigenous Jewish people).[24] In this type

---

24 The Khazars were a semi nomadic Turkic people who created the most powerful Western steppe empire, Khazaria, between the late seventh and tenth centuries. Beginning in the eighth century, the Khazar royalty and notable segments of the aristocracy converted to Judaism. A modern theory, claiming that the core of Ashkenazi Jewry emerged from a hypothetical Khazarian Jewish Diaspora, is generally faced with skepticism. (Wikipedia, s.v. "Khazars," last modified July 18, 2015, https://en.wikipedia. org/wiki/Khazars)

of country, there is no place for civil equality or partnership for other ethnic groups and religions. Just as in "Dar al-Islam," only in reverse, Arabs are protégés, are not considered to have full equal rights, and are therefore not equal citizens. This outlook has been passed down from first generation of immigrants to the second generation of native born Israelis and is prevalent among Sephardic Jews in Israel.

The National Religious Movement (Mizrahi) and Messianism

National Religious Jews emerged from the Yom Kippur War as a rising power of post-Zionism. The main source of their love for modern Israel is the messianic believe in the Bible verses that promise the return of the Jews at the end of days to their ancient homeland. This belief system has some surface similarities to the national secular movement, but the root is totally different. According to them, we were given this land by divine decree. Their belief rules out taking the approach making temporary concessions or using tactics that allow negotiations in consideration of other nations or of present-day empires. According to Zvi Yehuda Kook, who details the redemptive, mystical thinking of his father, Abraham Isaac Kook,[25] the main divine decrees of his (the son) teaching are speci-

---

25 Zvi Yehuda Kook (1891–1982) was a rabbi, leader of Religious Zionism, and Rosh Yeshiva of the Mercaz HaRav yeshiva. He was the son of Rabbi Abraham Isaac Kook. His teachings are partially responsible for the modern religious settlement movement in Judea and Samaria. Many of his ideological followers in the religious Zionist movement settled there. Under the leadership of Kook, with its center in the yeshiva founded by his father, Jerusalem's Mercaz HaRav, thousands of religious Jews actively campaigned against territorial compromise and established numerous settlements throughout the West Bank and Gaza Strip. Many of these settlements were subsequently granted official recognition by Israeli governments, both right wing and left. (Wikipedia, s.v. "Zvi Yehuda Kook," last modified July 9, 2015, https://en.wikipedia.org/wiki/Zvi_Yehuda_Kook) Abraham Isaac Kook (1865–1935) was the first Ashkenazi chief rabbi of the British Mandatory Palestine, the founder of the religious Zionist Yeshiva Mercaz HaRav Kook, and the religious Zionism denomination, Jewish thinker, Halakhist, Kabbalist and a renowned Torah scholar. He was one of the most celebrated and influential rabbis of the twentieth century. (Wikipedia, s.v. "Abraham Isaac Kook," last modified July 14, 2015, https://en.wikipedia.org/wiki/Abraham_Isaac_Kook)

fied in the commandments and actions for the redemption of the land. There is a detailed, practical reference to the Land of Israel as a center of gravity within a general outlook composed of three core values: the Torah (in this context this refers to all the Jewish teaching of national orthodox Jewry), the Land of Israel (aiming toward the Bible's promised land), and the biblical expression, the people of Israel, meaning the Jewish people.

Throughout the nation's history, there have been many instances of messianic ideology (religious belief in the *now* coming of the Messiah and the end of days) and of fundamentalist extremism. For example, the Sicariis,[26] the Sabbateans,[27] the Masada fundamentalists, and those battling the Hellenists[28]—these groups all brought about destruction, in various time periods, to the Jewish people. The messianic outlooks represent Judaism's mystical side, and those with these outlooks do not implement or listen to reason. They seem to possess both an exotic combination of charisma and an immediate solution to all our problems. In my conservative perception, this is the religious equivalent to the Peace Now movement. It is an inability to logically consider costs and alternatives, and it is determined by the emotional perception of the realness of the religious emergency situation in which we are supposed to find our

26   Sicarii zealots formed a Jewish extremist group active in the Judaea province in 6 AD. According to contemporary historian Josephus, following a zealotry rebellion when prominent Roman collaborators were killed, Judas of Galilee formed the Sicarii. This was a small and more extreme offshoot of the zealots. Their terror also was directed against Jewish collaborators, including temple priests, Sadducees, Herodians, and other wealthy elites.

27   Sabbateans (*Sabbatians*) is a complex general term that refers to a variety of followers of the disciples of Sabbatai Zevi (1626–76), a Jewish rabbi who was proclaimed in 1665 by Nathan of Gaza to be the Jewish Messiah. Vast numbers of people in the Jewish Diaspora accepted his claims, even after he became a Jewish apostate with his conversion to Islam in 1666. Sabbatai Zevi's followers, both during his Messiahship and after his conversion to Islam, are known as Sabbateans. (Wikipedia, s.v. "Sabbateans," last modified April 8, 2015, https://en.wikipedia.org/wiki/Sabbateans)

28   Hellenistic Judaism is a term describing the process by which Jews convert their culture, and at times their religion, to that of the Hellenistic culture, religion, language, and customs. Hellenism originated in ancient Greece.

world. This is the emotionally confused state of Atchalta De'Geulah (the outset of biblical redemption).

Most members of the Mizrahi movement are moderate in translating the Kook philosophy (of Kook the father and his son) into reality and are careful not to cross the line of national feasibility.[29] That is, because their political actions are not approved by the majority of society, they will accept contrary decisions made by the nation and the government. This behavior could be seen among settler leadership in 2005 when they were forced to evacuate their settlements in the Gaza Strip (the evacuation was completed in September that year). Most of them painfully accepted the evacuation despite clashing with their own set of values. Many of the settlers that belong to the Mizrahi movement openly justified their acceptance of the evacuation as a way to avoid creating a rift among the Jewish people and damaging the Israeli leadership's ability to govern. Despite all this, and due to this moderate outlook, some of the settlers with wide spiritual hold up among their youth and with the support of the spiritual rabbinical fringes, hold extreme beliefs of Atchalta De'Geulah,[30] and in it they find justification for aggravation and radicalization of religious decisions and rulings. For example, an increasing number of rabbis have made new rulings that overturn the objection of father and son Kook to pilgrimage to the Temple Mount. According to those new decrees, not only are Jews permitted to pray

---

29 Mizrahi (an acronym for Mercaz Ruhani, which means *religious center*) is the name of the religious Zionist organization founded in 1902 in Vilnius at a world conference of religious Zionists. According to Mizrahi, the Torah should be at the center of Zionism, and it sees Jewish nationalism as a means for achieving religious objectives. (Wikipedia, s.v. "Mizrahi" (religious Zionism), last modified February 12, 2015, https://en.wikipedia.org/wiki/Mizrachi_(religious_Zionism))

30 Atchalta De'Geulah (lit. "the beginning of the redemption") is a term for an idealistic concept derived from the Gemara. It refers to a new stage of revival in the process of the redemption and the coming of the Jewish Messiah. Hence, it is a pivotal point in time, because it is the initial stage of the salvation process that constitutes a different period in time, in many senses, and especially different from all previous period of times. It is the core idea of the Religious Zionism movement. (Wikipedia, s.v. "Atchalta De'Geulah," last modified June 4, 2014, https://en.wikipedia.org/wiki/Atchalta_De%27Geulah)

there, they are obligated to do so. Some of the extreme rabbis have also discussed pious rules related to gentiles. Those new discussions no longer address the religious circumstances for denying care and help to non-Jews but rather speak to when it is permitted to kill them.[31]

There is an increasing amount of messianic faith in holy writing and in the interpretation of the messianic rabbis as the absolute truth, completely disregarding actual physical reality. The thought is that whatever is seen as fact on the ground will change according to God's desires, especially on the basis of the written word in the new rabbis' teachings.

According to that extreme approach, burning fruit trees of non-Jews, stealing their property and vandalizing others' places of worship are not considered sins or transgressions, but steps accepted by Halakha among those committing these acts.[32] This constitutes an increase in the one-dimensional perception of the world with no distinction of layers or denominations. Regarding someone as either friend or foe is the common messianic approach. This radicalization can be seen in the uncompromising battle with fellow Jews whose religious approach is not messianic. Death threats given by religious extremist and threats on the property of moderate spokespeople even among the settlers themselves reached the point of removing and expelling moderate settlers from their home settlements, and deeming any different thought among those who remain in the settlements as invalid or treacherous. In the eyes of these extremist, if you choose to settle with them but hold a more moderate set of values, you enter a path with clear-cut consequences.

For generations Jews were not permitted to set foot on the holy mountain because of the lack of sufficient knowledge where the inner

---

31 Torat Hamelech, *Chapter One, The Laws Pertaining to Relations between Jews and non-Jews in Matters of Life and Death*, is a book of Halakha by rabbis Yitzhak Shapira and Yosef Elitzur the Od Yosef Chai (Yosef lives on) in Yitzhar. It primarily addresses law pertaining to killing non-Jews at times of both war and peace. The book was published in 2009. It opens with the core prohibition on killing non-Jews. It later addresses situations in which it is permitted and even suggested to kill non-Jews as punishment for not abiding by the Seven Laws of Noah as well as in times of war.

32 *Halakha* is the collective body of Jewish religious laws derived from the written and oral Torah.

sanctuary of the Temple was located. This was the holy room where the Ark of the Covenant with its ten commandments was kept during the First Temple. According to Jewish pious law, this secret holy place could only be entered by the High Priest once a year and was not to be contaminated with the touch of ordinary people. As mentioned and emphasized here, support of the pilgrimage to the Temple Mount for prayer demonstrates messianic fundamentalism that spreads in many parts of the National Religious population, and stands in opposition to the opinion expressed by father and son Kook. However, contemporary interpretation by some zealot rabbis pushes rapidly toward what they believe is the endgame of our world and the coming of the Jewish messiah.

The Effect of the Messianic Perspective on Broad Segments of the Jewish-Israeli Population

As claimed in the beginning of this chapter, the messianic perspective is occurring at a time of weakness for the Haredi movement. Neither modern-day versions of pious scholars like Rashi nor Rambam are with us as they used to in times of spiritual peak.[33] Less significant but still important, Avrohom Yeshaya Karelitz and Elazar Shach regrettably are also no longer with us.

This means that there is no contradictory leadership in the Haredi world to the messianic view. Likewise, the mediocrity of the Haredi knowledge, together with social and personal dogma accompanied with general ignorance, are fertile ground for spreading the one-dimensional messianic point of view in Israeli Haredi society.

Secularism, too, is facing one of its most challenging hours. The Yom Kippur War led the secular population to finally face the fact that their

---

33 Rabbi Shlomo Yitzchaki (1040–1105), presently known by the acronym RASHI, was a medieval French rabbi and the author of comprehensive commentary on the Talmud and the Old Testament. Moshe Ben Maimon, or Moses Maimonides, was a prominent medieval Sephardic Jewish philosopher and astronomer from Spain, and one of the most prolific and influential Torah scholars and physicians in the Middle Ages.

established state still stands, even when ambushed. This means that the Zionist main creation ended with an apparent success: a vital, sustainable state. However, the secular public was left with no leading ideology and no succeeding social values. The cultural and social fields were wide open to overseas influences like modern hedonism and Hellenism, and a consumer culture that meets the secular individual demands but disregards a huge hole in its soul. The essence of this hole is best presented in the natural need of many soldiers after the Yom Kippur War for an explanation as to why they survived while others died. It is also an irrational need for an irrational explanation of the nightmarish experience they just had during the war. All of this was accompanied with the growing lack of community support in a time of need. This spiritual support was always present among the religious population. These conditions serve as fertile ground for spreading messianic fundamentalism among the secular population as well, filling a hole in the cheap political aimed at the future rhetoric with present-day redemption, and offering the secular people a chance to take part in the community's efforts to revive and settle the old nation's lost territories of Judea and Samaria.

From the day of their immigration onward, the Sephardic Jewish population that moved to Israel (roughly twenty years before the war of 1973) as part of the melting pot creation and that of the new Jew, lost part of its traditional identity. This population primarily tended to see the secular Ashkenazi leadership and the Western secular society as an objective that one should strive to meet.

At the same time, partly as a means to avoid the blow to their psyche by being another rejected subculture, this part of the nation did not lose its traditional perspective, including the traditional longing for Zion. The idea of immigration to Israel as a realization of biblical prophecy, which warmed the hearts of most immigrants in the 1950s, also helped the Sephardic Jews from 1973 onward to form a natural, tradition-based bond between the Kooks' followers viewpoint and themselves. This bond was partially based upon the religious enthusiasm of mass immigrants of Middle Eastern descent. From this point onward, there is but a short distance for the messianic core ideas to make their way into the hearts of the many Jewish immigrants from these countries.

As far as the religious nationalist population was concerned, it was easily swayed by messianic thought because all its education led to the long-awaited moment of Atchalta De'Geulah, and the sooner the better.

Note that for reasons mostly unrelated to changes among the Jewish people but rather stem from internal Arab developments, the Arab communities turn to religion as well. Islam is becoming stronger among our Palestinian neighbors and our neighboring countries. The view of the Arab-Israeli conflict as a national conflict decreased with the decline of Nasserism and then even more with the death of Arafat.[34] Over the years, it gradually evolved into a pious Jewish-Muslim conflict over the Holy Land, similar to the conflict of the Muslims with the Christian crusaders. Therefore, the conflict between the Jewish and Palestinian people, as well as the conflict with the rest of the people in the region, has become more and more a religion-based conflict.

How It All Adds Up as Far as the Conflict between the Israelis and the Arabs: The Bottom Line

Al-Qaeda, Hamas, Hezbollah, and the Islamic movement in Israel are all sides of the same phenomenon of Pan-Islamism, which focuses on the resurrection of the old world of religious values as opposed to the sinister values of the West. Israel was built on Western values and ideas, and strives for material excellence and production efficacy according to Western-born ideology. From this point onward, it is a short distance for local Muslims, accustomed to Israel's Westernized context, to come to regard Zionism as a colonial/imperialistic, destructive force. Considering

---

34 Nasserism is a leftist Arab nationalist political ideology based on the thinking of Gamal Abdel Nasser, one of the two principal leaders of the Egyptian Revolution of 1952, and Egypt's second president. Spanning domestic and international spheres, it combines elements of Arab socialism, republicanism, nationalism, anti-imperialism, developing world solidarity and international nonalignment. (Wikipedia, s.v. "Nasserism," last modified July 13, 2015, https://en.wikipedia.org/wiki/Nasserism)

the religious radicalization of some of the Islamic fractions, the next logical and emotional step is short, and it brings Muslims to the concept of Jews as the new crusaders coming to desecrate Islam's holy places by just stepping a foot in Dar al-Islam.[35]

Since the 1980s, if one views the Arab-Israeli conflict through the spectacles of the Arabs, those who are considered successful in the combat against Zionism and the Jewish Israelis are those entities with religious motivation to defeat the Jews. Examples of such entities include the Sunni Hamas, who obtained and continue to hold the Gaza Strip in the face of the once Jewish settlers; and the Shiite Hezbollah, who twice expelled the Jewish IDF from Lebanese land. Even the crossing of the Suez Canal on Yom Kippur is appropriated by the Muslim Brotherhood for the heroics of the Egyptian believer and the army of believers.

The immediate consequence of this outlook is the inevitable conflict between twelve million Jews and billion and a half Muslims worldwide. The necessary result for Muslims is to regard Judaism as a religion only, with no national rights. Actually, this is going back to the times where Jews were being under the protection of Islam in all countries under its domain.

The immediate repercussion of the opposing Jewish messianic perspective is confrontation with the nations of the world, but primarily with Muslims, as they are perceived as attacking Jewish rights in the Promised Land and being the border violators of the divine decree.[36]

---

35 Dar al-Islam is a term used by Muslim scholars that refers to those countries where Muslims can practice their religion freely as the ruling sect. It pertains to territories under Islam rule: literally, "the home of Islam" or "the home of submission." These are usually Islamic cultures in which Muslims represent the majority of the population, and, therefore, the government promises them protection.
(Wikipedia, s.v. "Divisions of the world in Islam," last modified May 30, 2015, https://en.wikipedia.org/w/index.php?title=Divisions_of_the_world_in_Islam&redirect=no#Dar_al-Islam)

36 According to the Hebrew Bible, the covenant of the pieces or the covenant between the parts was a seminal event in the life of the biblical Patriarch. God revealed himself to Abraham and made a covenant with him, in which God announced to Abraham that his descendants would eventually inherit the land of Israel. This was the first of a series of covenants made between God and the Patriarchs. (Wikipedia, s.v. "covenant of the pieces," last modified February 2, 2015.)

The result is a religious confrontation with a cultural backdrop on a national basis: all three evils in one predominantly religious confrontation. In other words, a solution based on culture or nationalism will not end the conflict, and it is presently necessary to reach also a religious conclusions and agreements to firmly end the conflict.

For a demonstration of the abovementioned situation, it is sufficient to watch the handling of two groups of Israeli soccer fans during a match: the predominately Arab fans of Bnei Sakhnin and mainly Jewish fans of Beitar Jerusalem.[37] Another example may be seen in the way some rabbis rule against renting apartments to Arabs, coinciding with a fatwa that rules about not renting homes to Jews in Muslim towns.[38] The result is also evident in the way that graffiti has taken on an increasingly religious tone, painted by extremists on both sides on houses of prayer, cemeteries, and private property.

Even the ethical, religious justifications for killing people of the "other faith" (Torat Hamelekh, Halakha law regarding the killing of non-Jews, or fatwa permitting the killing of noncombat Jewish women and children) that have proliferated since the 1980s are proof of the end

---

37 Bnei Sakhnin F. C. (literally, *Sons of Sakhnin United*) is an Israeli football club based at the Doha Stadium in Sakhnin. They are the most successful Israeli-Arab club in the country, having won the State Cup in 2004. During a match with Beitar Jerusalem in September 2007, Beni Sakhnin supporters waved the flags of Syria and the green jihad flags of Islam. (Wikipedia, s.v. "Bnei Sakhnin F. C.," last modified July 19, 2015, https://en.wikipedia.org/wiki/Bnei_Sakhnin_F.C.) Beitar Jerusalem Football Club is an Israeli football club from Jerusalem and a member of the Israeli Premier League. The most vocal supporters of Beitar Jerusalem make up the controversial nationalist group La Familia. These fans are notorious for their hatred of Arabs and pride in the fact that Beitar Jerusalem is the only team in the IPL that has never included Arab players. Fans both inside and outside the stadium chant anti-Arab and racist slogans. The club has been penalized many times for its fans' behavior. (Wikipedia, s.v. "Beitar Jerusalem F. C.," last modified July 19, 2015, https://en.wikipedia.org/wiki/Beitar_Jerusalem_F.C.)

38 Fatwa, in the Islamic faith, is the term for the legal opinion or learned interpretation that a qualified jurist or mufti can give on issues pertaining to the Islamic law. This is not necessarily a formal position because most Muslims argue that anyone trained in Islamic law may give an opinion (fatwa) on its teachings. If a fatwa does not break new ground, then it is simply called a *ruling*. (Wikipedia, s.v. "Fatwa," last modified June 26, 2015, https://en.wikipedia.org/wiki/Fatwa)

result. This is also apparent in the increasing acceptance of incitement by religious leaders. For example, on Islam's side, Sheik Raed Salah spoke against all Jewish intent to destroy the Al-Aqsa Mosque,[39] and on the other side, extremist rabbis have urged prayer at the Temple Mount. Those on the fanatic sidelines have prepared themselves for dooms-day and for the way that, by divine decision, there will come an actual change to the physical characteristics of the Temple Mount (the Temple Institute).[40]

Summary

The Jewish perception of the state's power and the agreed toolbox of its leadership is a challenging one from the onset. From day one, Jews are told that we were all created in God's image. This means that not only were the leaders or the holders of senior positions created to be similar to their gods but also were the commoners. Due to this perception, the ruling classes in the Jewish nation have no birthright advantage upon their people. Unlike other system of believes in other regions, the Jewish ruling elites were not created specially to govern others. For its impor-tance to the understanding of this chapter I want to stress it once more: unlike gentile kings who possessed the divine right to rule, a right which is planted in their people's social and cultural substructure, Jews have a democratic viewpoint from the outset and claim that we were all created

---

39 Al-Aqsa Mosque is the third holiest site in Islam and is located in the old city of Jerusalem. The site on which the silver-domed mosque sits, along with the Dome of the Rock, also referred to as *al-Haram ash-Sharif* or Noble Sanctuary, is the Temple Mount, the holiest site in Judaism, the place where the Temple is generally accepted to have stood. (Wikipedia, s.v. "Al-Aqsa Mosque," last modified July 19, 2015, https://en.wikipedia.org/wiki/Al-Aqsa_Mosque)

40 The Temple Institute, known in Hebrew as *Machon HaMikdash*, is an organization in Israel focusing on the controversial endeavor of establishing the Third Temple. Its long-term aims are to build the third Jewish temple on the Temple Mount, the site currently occupied by the Dome of the Rock, and to reinstate sacrificial worship. (Wikipedia, s.v. "The Temple Institute," last modified July 11, 2014. https://en.wikipedia.org/wiki/The_Temple_Institute)

in his image; therefore, we are all equal. Furthermore, the Bible and Jewish tradition teach us to value and respect those who are different and do not fit into an accepted framework. Jewish heroes are those who rebel against authority to the point of rebuking God (as happened with both Abraham and Moses).[41]

Therefore, especially when an individual is brought up according to the teachings of Bar Kokhba and the prior revolt of Masada,[42] it is hard to expect that person to fully obey authority and understand the power and limitations of a modern nation-state. However, history will not let us off the hook without a twist. The period of the Judges is described as a period of chaos and disunity preventing effective handling of the biblical Philistine challenge.[43] This demonstrates the popular demand for strong governmental rule ("Now appoint a king to lead us," Samuel

41 When God told our forefather Abraham that he intended to destroy Sodom and Gomorrah, he presented God with an argument of ethics: "Shall not the Judge of all the earth do what is just?" He admonished God for the possibility of him committing the unjust act of destroying Sodom and Gomorrah. In the portion of Korach when the Jews as a collective people were at risk, Moses the prophet and his brother, Aaron, turned to God, who wanted to kill "this assembly...at once." Imploring God to show mercy, they said, "The God who gives breath to all living things, will you be angry with the entire assembly when only one man sins?"

42 Simon bar Kokhba (died 135 CE) was the Jewish leader of what is known as the Bar Kokhba revolt against the Roman Empire in 132 CE, establishing an independent Jewish state that he ruled for three years as *Nasi* (prince). His state was conquered by the Romans in 135 following a two-year war. Documents discovered in the modern era give us his original name, Simon ben Kosiba. He was given the surname Bar Kokhba (Aramaic for "Son of a Star," referring to the Star Prophecy of Numbers 24:17: "there shall step forth a star out of Jacob, and a scepter shall rise out of Israel, and shall smite through the corners of Moab") by his contemporary, the Jewish sage Rabbi Akiva. After the failure of the revolt, the rabbinical writers referred to bar Kokhba as "Simon bar Kozeba" ("Son of Lies" or "Son of Deception"). (Wikipedia, s.v. "Simon bar Kokhba," last modified May 20, 2015, https://en.wikipedia.org/wiki/Simon_bar_Kokhba)

43 The Book of Judges contains the history of biblical judges. These are divinely inspired leaders whose direct knowledge of God allows them to act as champions for the Israelites in fighting oppression by foreign rulers, and models wise and faithful behavior required by their God following the exodus from Egypt and the conquest of Canaan. The events of Judges are set between ca. 1380 CE and the rise of Saul, ca. 1050. (Wikipedia, s.v. "The Book of Judges," last modified July 25, 2015, https://en.wikipedia.org/wiki/Book_of_Judges)

1:8). Nonetheless, that monarchic rule that followed the time of judges had been proven to be faulty, and the repercussions caused a separation of kingdoms and eventually a two-thousand-year-long exile. During the exile, the Jewish people had to deal with the perceptions of their weakness against foreign leadership, rather than with the possibility of their self-governmental power equation.

Through all that, it is evident that strong governmental stability in a Jewish society is in and of itself a deep-rooted historical and cultural challenge. Classical Zionism strived to take Diaspora Jews, who had dealt with their gubernatorial weakness, and by using ethical and moral fortitude, attempted a retraining process that would fit them into the image of the Sabra (a Jew born in Israel), the new Jew. From Ahad Ha'am to A. D. Gordon and many others, an ethical, educational attempt was made to "form" innovative, confident Jews naturally reconnected to their land.[44] The Holocaust and corresponding historical events prevented the maturation of this kind of education among the majority of the Jewish people. The flood of refugees after the Holocaust from countries liberated from the Nazis consisted of Jews with Diaspora-like qualities. A generation that was meant to be the generation of the desert,[45] in an abrupt historical move, became the first generation to experience victory and self-governing power through self-government rule.

Sephardic Jews who had migrated to Israel were initially rejected by the ruling elite, and in turn, they rejected the concept of the changed Jew according to Zionism as well as the melting pot idea. In addition, the Sephardic Aliya in the 1950s was mostly not that of the Sephardic

---

44   Asher Zvi Hirsch Ginsberg (1856–1927), primarily known by his pen name, Ahad Ha'am (literally, *one of the people*, Genesis 26:10), was a Hebrew essayist and one of the foremost prestate Zionist thinkers. He is known as the founder of cultural Zionism. With his secular vision of a Jewish spiritual center in Israel, he opposed Theodor Herzl. Unlike Herzl, the founder of political Zionism, Ahad Ha'am strived for "a Jewish state and not merely a state of Jews." (Wikipedia, s.v. "Ahad Ha'am," last modified July 27, 2015, https://en.wikipedia.org/wiki/Ahad_Ha%27am)

45   This term refers to those who left Egypt but were not permitted by God to enter the Promised Land due to their scene of despair.

Jewish elite. The majority of the Sephardic best had chosen to emigrate to France or other countries (for example, Bernard-Henri Levy, an intellectual and author; Enrico Macias, a French Pied-Noir singer and musician; and Claude Cohen-Tannoudji, a physician and Nobel laureate). Therefore, Sephardic Jews who came to Israel have rejected Western Ashkenazi culture. Culturally, for the majority of Sephardic immigrants, the only remaining alternative from the time of the dramatic political shift in the 1977 election and onward was the popular version of their Sephardic culture seasoned with stories of Tzadiks (righteous Jews), holy water tales, and a deep high-culture abyss.[46]

This did not reflect upon the Jewish intellectual development of the Sephardic elite community, who, as previously stated, had chosen not to immigrate to Israel at all. Those who immigrated to Israel did not have a deep understanding of nationalism or had not brought with them a set of cultural tools of a national, democratic system of values. Processes of internalization made by the second generation since the time of mass Sephardi immigration were not yet complete, and the dramatic shift in government in 1977 had already taken place. The previously prevailing Western culture had been replaced by a Middle Eastern version of an alternative common culture.

Due to their crisis in values and leadership, the Haredi Jews are unable to adequately address the fact that there is a state governed by Jews. Therefore, they increasingly internalize the messianic perspective adopted by members of the Mizrahi movement. This process is happening mainly out of ignorance and disability to develop their own past view into a modern one. Hand in hand, a lacuna of spiritual leadership in the Haredi field is a major contributing factor.

---

46 The elections for the ninth Knesset were held on May 17, 1977. For the first time in Israeli political history, the right-wing Likud party won a majority in the Knesset, ending almost thirty years of rule by the left-wing Alignment and its predecessor, Mapai. The dramatic shift in Israeli politics caused by the outcome led to it becoming known as the dramatic change.

National Religious Jews are often guilty of hubris as they reiterate that they have almost singlehandedly realized the divine vision of re-settling the Promised Land and are convinced that inevitable success is part of their being, and not a passing phenomenon, as for the rest of us.

Throughout this, the internalization of a metaphysical and faith-based perception of the conflict that has existed for a hundred years has made this conflict more difficult to solve. It is worth asking whether it is at all possible to resolve the conflict through compro-mise in its current religious configuration. If the conclusion is that there is no peaceful solution, the immediate repercussion might be large-scale war involving 1.5 billion Muslims in opposition to 12 mil-lion Jews. In this scenario, it is interesting to note that the Jewish state, whose national secular origins had intended for it to be a place of refuge for the Jewish people, is inevitably becoming the source of uncompromising conflict of world Jewry with roughly a quarter of the world's population.

If a solution can be reached, can it be reached diplomatically, with the same old national leaderships? It may be necessary to con-sider having spiritual leaders connect and try to reach a religious solution based on sacred terminology. As a rule, this tactic requires the integration of religious dogma with the realm of interreligious negotiations. it does not appear that the natural place for concili-ation is in the realm of stubbornness. On the other hand, there is nothing quite like religious interpretation to pass the entire world through the eye of a needle, and it is possible that this is the true path to salvation.

A wonderful example from Judaism to the possibilities that do exist in a pious deliberation may be the old saying that women do not com-monly visit the Beth Din (house of judgment, Rabbinical Jewish Court). Well, it took a long-enough time, but nowadays for certain they do. If one should project from this example to the possibilities of spiritual so-lution rising among the settlers, then according to Rabbi Froman, "after all, they are there."[47] In other words, there are issues that are not ad-dressed in the Halakha, such as taking back the Promised Land from a section of its present occupants, who may be of Jewish blood.[48] Indeed, it is a place for creating a new and diverse Halakha-related literature with unpredictable results. suggest

The basic question "if an agreement can be reached?' is not only im-portant for the Jewish people, who are in the minority in comparison to the world of Islam. Christians and Confucians, as well as many Hindus and Buddhists, will observe the actions of Islam in this spiritual attempt to heal the conflict and decide whether to consider taking defensive or aggressive steps toward some fractions of Islam, in accordance with what

---

47 Rabbi Menachem Froman (1945–2013) was an Israeli Orthodox Jewish rabbi, a peacemaker and negotiator with close ties to Palestinian religious leaders from the PLO and Hamas. A founding member of Gush Emunim, he served as the chief rabbi of Tekoa in the West Bank. He was well known for promoting and leading interfaith dialogue between Israeli Jews and Palestinians, focusing on using religion as a tool and source for recognizing the humanity and dignity of all Palestinians. Together with a Palestinian journalist close to Hamas, Rabbi Froman drafted a cease-fire agreement known as the Froman-Amayreh Agreement, between Israel and the Hamas government in the Gaza Strip. The agreement was endorsed by Hamas but has yet to receive any official response from the Israeli government. (Wikipedia, s.v. "Menachem Froman," last modified May 9, 2015, https://en.wikipedia.org/wiki/Menachem_Froman) In response to a question about the divine decree (the will of God to give the Promised Land to the Jews), he ended his argument by saying that they (the Palestinians) are there.

48 Israel Belkind, the founder of the Bilu movement, also asserted that Palestinian Arabs were the blood brothers of the Jews. In his book on Palestinians, *The Arabs in Eretz-Israel*, Belkind advanced the idea that the dispersion of Jews out of the land of Israel following the destruction of the Second Temple by the Roman emperor Titus is an er-ror of historic proportions that must be corrected. Whereas much of the land's Jewish community dispersed around the world, those "workers of the land that remained at-tached to their land" stayed behind and were eventually converted to Christianity and then to Islam. (Wikipedia, s.v. "Israel Belkind," last modified April 27, 2015, https://en.wikipedia.org/wiki/Israel_Belkind)

Tsvi Misinai, an Israeli researcher, entrepreneur, and proponent of a controversial alternative solution to the Israeli-Palestinian conflict, asserts that nearly 90 percent of all Palestinians living within Israel (including the Bedouin Negev) are descended from the Jewish Israelite peasantry that remained on the land after the others, mostly city dwellers, were exiled or left behind. (Wikipedia, s.v. "Tsvi Misinai," last modified May 27, 2015, https://en.wikipedia.org/wiki/Tsvi_Misinai)

they have observed. The motivation to reach a solution exists on both moderate sides of the equation.

As far as I'm concerned, if a peaceful solution that demands compromise is ever found, then as a Jew and as a Zionist, I believe there is another important issue at hand that demands attention: how to bring all messianic Jews "back home" to middle-of-the-stream moderate pious perception, with as little pain, sorrow and anguish as possible. Many of us are not interested in a crisis of faith to such an important part of our people. If such an event will ever take place, it would be obviously advised to ease the pain of losing the paradigm and reduce the aftershock for the younger generation. Special Halakha work should be prepared for such circumstances by the spiritual leaders of the National Religious Jews, perhaps even by people of faith who are not of their sect, in order to allow them to climb out of their place of heartbreak toward a warm, comforting existence. As a Zionistic Jew, I, too, am obligated to teach everyone I know to lovingly accept our "now-radical" and future to-be-heartbroken brethren. False interpretation of history is not their fault. We all walk this road together, and we continue to bear the past and present burden. Despite all their flaws, the tribes of Yehudah, Israel, and Erev Rav are united.[49]

49 Erev Rav is the name of an inclusive group containing Egyptians and other peoples who accompanied the Israelites on their exodus from Egypt. According to Jewish tradition, they were accepted by Moses as an integral part of the nation.

CHAPTER 5:

CATALYSTS CAUSING THE FURTHER LOSS OF VALUES IN ISRAEL

About the Culture of Deceit and the Screen of Hatred

*Though much is taken, much abides; and though
we are not now that strength which in old days
Moved earth and heaven, that which we are, we are...*
—*Alfred, Lord Tennyson*, Ulysses

Introduction

In his book *The Guide for the Perplexed*, Maimonides teaches readers that there are parts of faith that we are obliged to express and protect, even if they not properly established, all of that in order to preserve a nation's frameworks of life and its security.[50] In my opinion, Maimonides was

---

50 *The Guide for the Perplexed* is one of the major works of Rabbi Moshe ben Maimon, better known as Maimonides or "the Rambam." It was written in the twelfth century in the form of a three-volume letter to his student, Rabbi Joseph ben Judah of Ceuta, the son of Rabbi Judah, and is the main source of the Rambam's philosophical views, as opposed to his opinions on Jewish law. Because many of the philosophical concepts, such as his view of theodicy and the relationship between philosophy and religion, are relevant beyond strictly Jewish theology, it has been the work most commonly associated with Maimonides in the non-Jewish world, and it is known to have influenced several major non-Jewish philosophers. Following its publication, "almost every philosophic work for the remainder of the Middle Ages cited, commented on, or criticized Maimonides's views." Within Judaism, the *Guide* became widely popular, with

right, as was Plato, who argued that sometimes leaders need to lie about things concerning the foundations of society's existence.[51] For me, the hypocrisy that seems always connected to the leading social classes is quite necessary in order to preserve the order of any regime and its administration in this chaotic world. Yet in Israel, it took a different path. Contrary to what other countries did, and also due to the immediate need for myths and ethos appropriate for the newly formed Jews, the early leadership in Israel did tend to adopt and assume as their own the admiration of the masses and turn victories in battle into mythical victories achieved by bigger than life leaders. The challenge was that some of those heroic figures were still active in the leadership's arena.

If you ascribe miracles and marvels on the national level to a person who is still alive and functioning as part of your leading elite, then there is a great chance that he shall be erroneous on one of his next moves (e.g., the 1973 October War). In such case, the masses realize that the mask parade has stopped; and at the end, lies are bound to be revealed. This chapter aims to discuss one of the sore evils of the Israeli society:[52] the culture of hatred that has developed through the moral crisis following the exposure of governmental lies.. Even though the perpetual sensation among many young, educated citizens of Israel toward its political leadership is that of "dwarves on the shoulders of giants"; even though whatever they (Maimonides and Plato) managed to summarize in one

---

many Jewish communities requesting copies of the manuscript, but also quite controversial, with some communities limiting its study or banning it altogether. (Wikipedia, s.v. *"The Guide for the Perplexed,"* last modified July 5, 2015, https://en.wikipedia.org/wiki/The_Guide_for_the_Perplexed)

51   Plato was a philosopher in classical Greece. He was also a mathematician, student of Socrates, writer of philosophical dialogues, and founder of the Academy in Athens, the first institution of higher learning in the Western world. Along with his mentor, Socrates, and his most famous student, Aristotle, Plato helped to lay the foundations of Western philosophy and science. (Wikipedia, s.v. "Plato," last modified July 27, 2015, https://en.wikipedia.org/wiki/Plato)

52   *Sore evil* is a public norm or a social phenomenon that is initially spoiled, is difficult to uproot, and is inherently broken (as per Ecclesiastes 5:13: "There is a sore evil *which* I have seen under the sun, *namely,* riches kept for the owners thereof to their hurt").

sentence, we in the present generation need a book to explain; I shall attempt to specify, if only a little and mainly for the benefit of the reader who still is devoid of this knowledge.

The Culture of Deceit

Just as in any other country, changes in Israel that would meet the needs of the public are prevented by built-in obstructions in the public's behavior. In extreme situations, some of these obstructions even act as catalysts for tremendous development up to the point in which these injure the stability of the state.

One of these catalysts is the local culture of deceit. My claim is that the source of that culture is the encounter between the Zionist theory and the reality in the land of Israel, and the breakthrough of the public insight occurred during the crisis that revealed the truth following the Yom Kippur War (in October 1973).[53] Despite the wish to create a new Israeli-Jewish person, the governmental and cultural elite of the evolving state of Israel were on a tight schedule. Time wise, there was a narrow window of opportunity to achieve many needed cultural creations. After all, an attempt to restore a nation after two thousand years of exile takes a lot of doing. As a result, they settled for what they had, and they declared that Jews who come back to the motherland should aspire to achieve the characteristics of the Sabra. The validity of the mythological Sabra's existence was never examined. He was the image of the pioneer with the splendid mane who when was hungry "borrowed" chickens from the Kibbutz chicken coop. (Of course the "borrowing" was not called by its proper name, theft, and was never considered as such but only as childish naughtiness of young men who were leaving the next day for the battlefield, and no one knew if or when they might return).

---

53 The Yom Kippur War, also known as the 1973 Arab-Israeli War, was fought by the coalition of Arab states led by Egypt and Syria against Israel from October 6 to October 25, 1973. (Wikipedia, s.v. "Yom Kippur War," last modified July 18, 2015, https://en.wikipedia.org/wiki/Yom_Kippur_War)

As one who has a straight shooter personality, he was the one who talked directly rather than "circumambulate" as Diaspora Jews did. The Sabra Jew was heroically portrayed as one who on a day of war could look straight into the eyes of his enemy without flinching yet was sufficiently bighearted to make peace with that enemy on the next day.

The actual purity-of-arms concept that was created around the same time as the Sabra was a problematic notion even in those days.[54] After all, war is hell, and as such, it exhausts itself as fire in a thorn field. Had war been a good thing, nations around the world would have fought even more. There is no purity in fighting for its own sake, but only the need to fight for defense and for achieving political and other goals using the language of power.

Following the establishment of the Israeli state, the Mapai members,[55] who were aware of the gap between the world of values that they tried to introduce and the actual reality, nevertheless supported spreading lies in order to fortify the nation's morale and yet advance the values that they favored. No one discussed the impediments or flaws these kinds of talks were left for the opposition.

---

54 The *purity of arms* code is one of the values stated in the Israel Defense Forces' official doctrine of ethics, *The Spirit of the IDF*. According to Norman Solomon, the concept of purity of arms arose out of the ethical and moral values stemming from the tradition of Israel, extrapolation from the Jewish Halakha, and the desire for moral approval and hence political support from the world community. Despite doubts when confronted by indiscriminate terrorism, purity of arms remains the guiding rule for the Israeli forces. These foundations have elicited a fair degree of consensus among Jews, both religious and secular. Detractors of the Israeli army challenge this image, notably in the light of certain harsh actions and massacres that have marked the army's history. According to Gideon Levy, the "majority of the Israelis is still deeply convinced that their army, the IDF, is the most moral army of the world, and nothing else." (Wikipedia, s.v. *"purity of arms,"* last modified June 8, 2015, https://en.wikipedia.org/wiki/Purity_of_arms)

55 Mapai (literally "Workers' Party of the Land of Israel") was a left-wing political party in Israel, and was the dominant force in Israeli politics until its merger into the modern-day Israeli Labor Party in 1968. During Mapai's time in office, a wide range of progressive reforms was carried out, as characterized by the establishment of a welfare state, providing minimum income, security, and free (or almost free) access to housing subsidies and health and social services. (Wikipedia, s.v. "Mapai," last modified July 28, 2015, https://en.wikipedia.org/wiki/Mapai)

The Zionist-Socialist mission of the time was not completed yet, and while it was being built, the muses were silent. Of course, at the same time, the leadership's ideas were reflected also through the major trends of culture and communication. But in reality, the leadership strayed more and more from a desired elite behavior to the edges of morally wrongs and the fringes of legality These are some of the more famous examples: if a certain personality chose to "adopt" some of the state's precious archeological articles, it was considered "borrowing"; if a certain personality did cross the lines and maybe even the rules of criminal law in his attitude toward his secretary or a woman he encountered at a party, such issues were silenced as an act of naughtiness in which the woman was considered to be the one who encouraged him either through her attire or social manners. There was almost no escape from the public pretense. Prime Minister Eshkol's stuttering during his famous speech on the radio was one human anomaly in the flow of pretenses and white lies by the leadership.[56] The early compositions of Ephraim Kishon, who throughout the years was considered to side with the ideas of the right-wing Zionism and by using humor and piercing satire tried to reveal what was behind the screen of leadership hypocrisy, acted only as a passing episode and eventually caused him to be continuously pushed out of the major cultural stage.[57]

The catharsis was reached after the Six-Day War. Every politician was considered as godlike, and every general was half a deity. Pictures of politicians and members of IDF's general staff were distributed and hung everywhere, and victory albums were sold and distributed all over. The pure little Israel had defeated its enemy in six days! Regarding its

---

56   Levi Eshkol (1895–1969) served as the third prime minister of Israel from 1963 until his death from a heart attack in 1969. He was the first Israeli prime minister to die in office. Today, Eshkol's intransigence in the face of military pressure to launch an Israeli attack is considered to have been instrumental in increasing Israel's strategic advantage as well as in obtaining international legitimacy, yet at the time he was perceived as hesitant, an image cemented following a stuttered radio speech on May 28. (Wikipedia, s.v. "Levi Eshkol," last modified July 11, 2015, https://en.wikipedia.org/wiki/Levi_Eshkol)

57   Although Kishon was a popular Israeli writer, he still felt he was getting negative treatment from the Israeli media because he was rather right-wing politically.

proportions, it was almost a biblical kind of miracle. However, it was a Mapai-Zionistic leadership, so distribution of partial lies about the honor code, resourcefulness and glory of the new Sabra and glorification of his leaders were considered necessary.

At this point, I wish to emphasize again that deification of mythical figures and cultural hypocrisy is a vital part in every ruling method. The problem with the young Israel at the end of the 1960s and beginning of the 1970s was, of course, that the generals and politicians—who were glorified as semi-gods or gods—were still alive and active, while in other cultures, such figures are historical ones, and there is no other proof that may contradict the myth woven about them. Someone in the young state of Israel had forgotten that the board game may and will change and then it may expose these alleged heroes in their nakedness.

In narrow retrospect, the War of Attrition following the 1967 war did justify in retrospect the glorification of the Six-Day War, but nothing lasts forever. The social voices, which were previously castrated, started to raise their heads. They included the Black Panthers, the Bourekas Films,[58] *Kazablan*,[59] and the Yerida phenomenon (up to the point of the famous

---

58   The Bourekas films were a genre of Israeli-made movies popular in Israel in the 1960s and 1970s. Film critic Uri Klein describes Bourekas films as a "peculiarly Israeli genre of comic melodramas or tearjerkers...based on ethnic stereotypes." They were "home-grown farces and melodramas that provided escapist entertainment during a tense period in Israeli history." The term is said to have been coined by the Israeli film director Boaz Davidson, the creator of several such films, as a play on words on the "spaghetti western" genre, known as such because that particular Western subgenre was produced in Italy. Bourekas is also a notable dish from Israeli cuisine. (Wikipedia, s.v. "Bourekas films," last modified January 2, 2015, https://en.wikipedia.org/wiki/Bourekas_film)

59   *Kazablan* is an early Israeli Hebrew language play, staged first as a 1954 drama, followed by a 1964 screen adaptation, later as a 1966 musical comedy, and still later produced as a 1974 musical comedy film. The name Kazablan comes from *Casablanca*, the birthplace of the main character. The musical's huge success made what was then a "young Jerusalem-born singer" Yehoram Gaon "not only...an overnight singing star, but also a figure of solidarity and pride for people of Sephardic origin, many of whom were entering a theatre for the first time." Gaon later reprised his role in the film version. (Wikipedia, s.v. "Kazablan," last modified February 9, 2015, https://en.wikipedia.org/wiki/Kazablan)

joke: the last one to leave the airport (immigrating abroad) must turn off the light)[60]—all these were insinuating that the end of an era was coming.

The time of lies ended with the Yom Kippur War (the 1973 October War). The mask was abruptly torn off the faces of the leaders, and the anxious nation discovered that its leaders were human beings just like us, with weaknesses and needs. Thousands of warriors found out that they and their colleagues and all the citizens of the state had paid the price for the governmental cover up and the lies told by the leadership. The previously familiar scene of the culture world and press being led astray for the sake of the leadership's needs will never be repeated again. Questions were asked and passed around and then reached the city squares and the press. Books and plays were formed in the minds of writers and presented the Israeli as less sacred and more humane. The sacred cows that acted as defensive barriers[61]—for example, the expression "state security" as a hush code in any conversation—were retreating, and the public self-employed censorship was gradually losing its power.

The first one to break through was the religious power of the National Religious wing, which set out on what was initially an illegal settlements momentum contrary to the wishes of some elements in the political leadership.[62] This gave wind under the wings of some suppressed and obviously enraged ethnic groups and caused the famous political upheaval of 1977.[63]

---

60 *Yerida* is a Hebrew term referring to emigration by Israeli Jews from the state of Israel. Yerida is the opposite of Aliyah (literally "ascent"), which is immigration to Israel. Zionists are generally critical of the act of *yerida,* and the term is somewhat derogatory. Common reasons for emigration are economic constraints, criticism of the government, lack of security due to ongoing Palestinian political violence and the Arab-Israeli conflict, perceived religious coercion and academic or professional advancement. (Wikipedia, s.v. "Yerida," last modified July 20, 2015, https://en.wikipedia.org/wiki/Yerida)

61 *Sacred cows* is a Hebrew expression relating to issues that are not to be questioned.

62 Israeli settlements in the territories of Judea and Samaria.

63 The elections for the ninth Knesset were held on May 17, 1977. For the first time in Israeli political history, the right wing, led by Likud, won a plurality in the Knesset, ending almost thirty years of rule by the left-wing Alignment and its predecessor, Mapai. The dramatic shift in Israeli politics caused by the outcome led to it becoming known as "the (Political) Turnover."

The leadership upheaval in the people's consciousness that started at the end of the Yom Kippur War also generated by itself a change in the culture of deceit—no more acceptance of ideological or governmental dogmas. The public's trust in the assertions of authority or government figures has decreased so much in the course of time that at present, if someone declares the intention of becoming a political leader or a politician, it is considered admittance that up to some degree he or she is a liar. Regrettably, the representatives of the executive authority have gained the same reputation.

After the end of the Yom Kippur War, military people were also investigated with greater severity if they had made any mistake of oversight that had cost human lives. The heads of the police were required to present an account regarding the policemen's behavior toward civilians in the after war protests. Currently, the police are so mistrusted that seemingly almost no one but the judge believes the statements of policemen or security men in court.

The same is true regarding members of the state prosecution. The public regards them basically as biased liars who only defend their colleagues and social pairs at the expense of the public. Derogatory nicknames for them have already turned into common ones on the street and the net. From there, it was a short road to the loss of trust in the powers of homeland security and the partial to total lack of cooperation with them.

This loss of public trust in government leaders and officials was not the only result of the Yom Kippur War. In an odd twist, the culture of deceit was translated into the individual's levels and turned into prevalent one on the personal individual level. As soon as the fighting subsided, it seemed as though the Israeli citizens were telling themselves, "If the leaders lied to me up to the point of causing life-threatening situations and endangering the country, then I too can lie for my own individual benefit." "I won't let them use me as a sucker anymore," said the individual and started what in a later perspective seems to be the beginning hers or his moral deterioration.

The state of affairs at present is such that almost all kinds of lies are acceptable in the public's domain, and for parts of the population, some lies are not even considered morally wrong any more. To be perfectly clear, I would like to point out that I am not referring to a farmer who hides some of his products from the tax collector. I am not talking about lies that are related to sabotaging transactions between the citizen and the authorities who are demonstrating their power. Nor am I referring to problematic relations in the field due to disagreements about authority between the local rule and the national one. All these kinds of evasions and power demonstrations do exist in Israel, just as in any other society.

The difference is that the Israeli citizen per se acts like he is no longer obliged to ever tell the truth. It seems as though he says, "If the entire system is corrupt and everybody is lying, why should I be the one who is always suffering because of my honesty?" Hence, the large reference to the ever increasing misusage of National Insurance, by all society levels, as a legitimate financial source. That is why citizens feel it is not necessary to be precise about the truth. Obviously that kind of deceit cloture causes immediate implications for the private insurance industry, false declarations given to the police or in court ruin the trust in the judicial authority and its trust in the value of spoken evidence given in a court of law. Finally, the bogus tales of soldiers to their commanders in the army or to their employers in civilian life ruins possibilities for improvements in both the civilian and military sectors.

The Effects of the Culture of Deceit on the State's Institutions

On a person's day-to-day level, the culture of deceit has no boundaries and apparently has spilled into all areas of personal life—from the numbers and types of lies told at work to the numbers and types of divorces requested. However, this is not the angle of observation in this present passage.

As a rule, the single lie one makes to the authorities encourages double expenditure. There are actual profits that the citizen receives unlawfully from the state's institutions (including disability allowance, nursing services, various types of supports, and so on). These result in some citizens not being given whatever is due to them because the amounts allocated for that were already drawn from the public's register. And because of the increasing fraud, a system of control and follow-up was widened, and its costs are also partly responsible for more missing funds.

Civil servants and authorities have also adopted the rules of the culture of deceit, and rarely, if ever, correct their mistakes for the sake of the future. Every department manager, senior clerk or elected official denies any involvement with mistakes being done or challenges in their institutions and would rather tell a lie than face the consequences or contribute to the greater good. It is important to understand that in such a social atmosphere, each fraud that was possible and necessary to investigate upon and draw conclusions from will either not be examined or will not be inspected properly. Because it would be impossible to find truth speakers, we will never learn the lessons that are required to fix the system and its mistakes.

On the highest level, most of today's elected politicians do comprehend that they are expected to lie, which is why they feel no obligation to stand behind the groups that helped them win the leadership. Following the elections, most of them may pay lip service regarding their campaign promises while at the same time enact policies that correlate with their personal interests. Following such acts, not only the leader's reliability but the integrity of the entire public sphere disappears, and with it also the basic honesty of civilians.

Within such an atmosphere, the civilian who has integrity and believes in telling the truth is like a victim waiting for his hangman. Very few civilians would agree to place themselves in such a position and endanger their achievements and the well-being of their families for the sake of values and public standards that are perceived as old fashioned or as mere things.

Those Who Benefit and Those Who Lose through Such Culture

The main winners are the people of fortune and authority who are not obliged to anyone or anything, who lack integrity or do not feel obliged to admit any errors or to provide some required economic payment to correct any wrongs. The members of this thin layer of society are aggrandizing their profits and strength at the expense of the general public's truth.

The people in this very limited layer also have the best integrity advocates (public relations experts) that money and power can buy, and these advocates handle the lies and defamation for them. The simple citizen has no chance in a public or judicial struggle against them. The system in Israel (as I suspect in many other places) always supports and stands behind its senior figures. Citizens who complain or attempt to fight an unfair situation by leading a demonstration or turning to the court will wear out their own public images. Partly because of the money and recourses that would be carefully contributed (especially for the purpose of smear campaign by public relations agents hired by the rich and powerful), such citizens would be regarded as troublemakers in court and would be ridiculed by top prosecutors and defense attorneys who would be glad to defend the government's and upper-circle's representatives in exchange for some publicity and collaboration.

Thus, there is no importance to any declaration of intent or a priori promise by the head of a corporation or a prime minister. All that matters is when they decide to come out to the public and announce the so-called victory over the hostile elements. All of it, including the way it is done and the timing, is in the eyes of the Israeli public a derivative of personal momentary conjecture.

The main people who are injured are members of the general public who regard their world and their country as precious. Nevertheless, there is nothing they can do at present to prevent the situation. Citizens' sense of security in their homes has declined, and because more and more citizens do not collaborate freely with the "bad police," the only other people who profit from this situation are the outlaws and the underworld members. The current state of affairs is referred to in public as "might makes right."[64]

This situation does not enable learning through mistakes, which is why the state as well as the corporations or the companies it owns (postal services, national power grid, water authorities, roads and transportation, and so on) are weakening persistently, precisely in those areas where repair and correction are needed.

At best, this failure to fix problems results in a decline in the state-owned corporation's competitiveness and an increase in losses. This, in turn, damages the balance sheets of the pension funds and investment portfolios that belong to members of the public. In the worst case, it means a future dismissal of hundreds and thousands of employees or, in worst scenario, oversight of this challenge by the state until a whole generation is left without basic pension fees, which might cause violent social eruptions that cost lives of soldiers, firefighters, prison guards, and ordinary citizens.

The Screen of Hatred and the Celebration of Ignorance

As in any other modern country, Israel has currents of seclusion (segregation) and difference that run in parallel to the national ethos and myth aimed at uniting the citizens around the state and its existing values. The difference is in the multiplicity of the rifts and the blowing at the flames that is done by interested elements.

The clear rift is between Arabs and Jews, and this hatred is expressed everywhere. It begins with the spiritual adjudications of the community leaders on both sides of the barricades, the Muslim and the Jewish, who prohibit renting or selling houses to each other. It continues through

---

64 "Might makes right" is a phrase that originated in the Babylonian Talmud and refers to cases in which there is no way for the court to clarify the truth, so the person who has power wins. Nowadays the term describes a violent society in which the decision is made according to considerations of power only, ignoring the values of morality and justice.

the fanning of the flames in competitions between sports groups. Perhaps the worst manifestation of this hatred is that where the legitimacy of democratic elections won through the votes of the minority that politically joined with one side of the majority is doubted. The losing party always claims that the victory was stolen from it or deviously stolen through collaboration with the Arab minority, that the losing party considers the enemy within.

The other rift is between the Ashkenazi and the Sephardic. Their hatred is best expressed on the media and through Internet talkbacks through the use of words and expressions such as "The Sephardic are like Arab monkeys," "Khazars," and "The Ashkenazi are seeds of annihilation."

The hatred between the left wing and the right wing has been added to these two rifts. It relates mainly to what most of the Jewish citizens perceive as "leftist liberal ideas" of peace and coexistence. The so-called blessings exchanged between these two factions range from slurs such as "traitor who should be sentenced to death" for the common leftist to "fascist, Nazi baboon" for the rightist.

There is also the hatred between the secular and the religious and especially between the extreme orthodox and the secular. In this case, the mutual exchange of blessings include insults such as "Nazi," used by the orthodox, and "Doss" or "black penguins," used by the secular.[65]

Another kind of hatred exists between the groups of newcomers from Ethiopia ("monkeys," as they are called by those who hate them) and the newcomers from the former USSR (called "nach" by the Ethiopians). Antagonism also exists between the senior immigrants and the newcomers and is expressed through the description of those born in Israel as "barbaric," the newcomers from Russia as "mafia" and "whores and pimps," and those from Ethiopia as "bearers and distributers of illnesses."

---

65 *Doss* is a disrespectful Hebrew slang word used to describe an extreme Orthodox Jew. The term *black penguins* is a derogatory reference to the traditional attire of the extreme Orthodox.

New hatreds have evolved in the last few years toward foreign work-ers and the stream of African infiltrators, many of whom are seeking work while others seek asylum. Nicknames such as "fifth column" or "enemies of the state" are some of the less derogative ones ascribed to the Africans.

Then there is the hatred between the poor and the rich and espe-cially hatred of those who are perceived by many as members of the corrupted "fortune and authority" circle. Their nicknames include "cor-rupted" and "criminals," which so far, seem to satisfy the masses.

The problem is not in the rifts and not even in their multiplicity, but in the fact that these rifts are common for the entire population (namely, all hate all accordingly). Consequently, these rifts act as excel-lent incubators for ignorance and the lack of comprehension of those one tends to hate, which leads to the weakening of the social and human tapestry that composes this state.

If you are a Sephardic Jew with religious orientation, and you are also poor, you will hate the Ashkenazi Jews whose parents brought your parents to the country, humiliated them at the "absorption camps," and presently, as the highest social class, prevent you from making progress in this world. But they are not the only ones you hate: many of the sec-ular Israelis are considered in your eyes as "haters of Israel," and the Arabs are considered as its "Amalek" (mythological strongest enemy); the newcomers from the former Soviet Union are "the enemy from with-in," and the Ethiopians are "not clean" and are "carrying diseases," and basically, there are doubts about their Judaism. There are also doubts about the Judaism of the Ashkenazi Jews, who apparently originated from the Khazars. As a Sephardic, you claim that generally, all the rich (supposedly Ashkenazi) people are suffocating you; all the nations in the world are against you as a Jew. Just look at their latest representa-tives, the work-seeking immigrants who came to "blacken" our streets and neighborhoods.

If, for example, you are a secular Christian Arab who is economically well established, then you will hate the Muslim Arabs who humiliated you as a Christian in Dar-El-Islam. You will loathe the Jews for discriminating against you and the newcomers because they are being promoted at work before you are. You will hate the work-seeking immigrants for taking away your son's possible place of work, the religious ones who impose a life of faith upon all, and the lazy masses who threaten everything you managed to achieve by yourself.

This is how it goes on and on for almost each and every one of us. In Israel, we are not educated to "love thy neighbor" or the person who is different. So far, in such a varied country, there are no successful educational programs designed to help us think about and accept differences, which should be in the center of the core studies in the country and in all its educational sectors.

Those Who Profit the Most from This Situation

Naturally, this kind of situation encourages sectarian politicians and spiritual leaders to fan the fire between the held rifts, even to the point of inciting violence and damaging the state's texture. In addition to those politicians who gain the support of the incited masses, easily by some assertion, the rich people also benefit from this state in which there is no organized and unified opposition of citizens, either working employees or buying customers. For example, during the big demonstrations of the Israeli Summer of Protest in the summer of 2011, there were not many Arabs, foreign workers, or Haredi Jews among the protestors (despite the fact that they constitute the weakest populations, and even though one of the successful leaders of the protest was a Haredi Jew). Contrary to that, some may say that this social protest was the call of the middle class, but there is a middle class also among the Arabs and Orthodox Jews, so why they were not viewed on the streets?

Due to the polarization and hatred, during the past few decades there have been no demonstrations by workers that contained all or even most of the groups in the population as they exist in the social map. The general strike was a weapon whose legitimacy was worn out by the public relations agents of the rich and people in authority, who claimed that the damage by such a strike may reach the people's threshold, and in all cases by using this doomsday weapon, all is lost and nothing is gained. In fact, until the Summer of Protest (in 2011), all the workers' unions did was conduct rearguard battles, following the common widespread approach according to which the unions are an example of the "power to corrupt." Following this well-funded and publicized approach, the mainstream wisdom praised the personalized working agreements and the high-tech world's work relations.

Moreover, the rich and powerful social ring also realized that using the road of inner division and hostility made their work easier. Thanks to the separatism, the current social-economic development offered by the state is mainly divided into sectors according to social affiliation. Worse than that, the plans are executed by the political representatives of the various sectors, based on what is mostly viewed as done at the expense of others.

Rehabilitation of neighborhoods in the periphery is promoted by the Likud or Shas parties,[66] which are perceived by most Israelis (excluding the Ethiopians) as the saviors or at least patrons of the people from Muslim countries (Sephardic). The rehabilitation of poor settlements inhabited by Mizrachi followers will be taken care of by their representatives in the

---

66 Likud is the major center-right party in Israel. A secular party, it was founded in 1973 by Menachem Begin in an alliance with several right-wing and liberal parties. Likud's victory in the 1977 elections was a major turning point in the country's political history, marking the first time the left had lost power. In addition, it was the first time in Israel that a right-wing party won the plurality of the votes. (Wikipedia, s.v. "Likud," last modified July 25, 2015, https://en.wikipedia.org/wiki/Likud) *Shas* is an ultraorthodox religious political party in Israel. Founded in 1984 under the leadership of Rabbi Ovadia Yosef, a former Israeli Sephardi chief rabbi, who remained its spiritual leader until his death in October 2013, it primarily represents the interests of Haredi Sephardic Jews. (Wikipedia, s.v "Shas," last modified July 20, 2015, https://en.wikipedia.org/wiki/Shas)

Knesset[67]—after these are part of the government—and they will do so by allocating designated funds from the general budget. The general budget is divided by sectors, which imply that what we extra pay for one sector is taken from the sum dedicated to others. The representatives of the ultraorthodox would act the same and see to their own people. Because there is no governmental perception of the society as one and what is or isn't a true, wide, public economic issue, all would suffer from weakness of the social framework, and eventually all governmental efforts would have limited impact only, if any at all.

However, neither the politicians nor the wealthy people relate or even support any declared united agenda or promotion of inclusive programs. For them, the immediate political profit is only by investing in sectarian politics. The more the public is divided in these ways, the easier it is for the shrewd politician—who establishes himself through hatred—to inflame his tribe of voters to vote for him. For the wealthy, a public that is divided and weak is preferable, as this sort of public accepts products (all or whatever is given to it) without the ability for organized protest. In the meanwhile, the public that is working for the firms and companies owned by the wealthy ones is afraid of the pressure from other external people who want to work at any cost, and thus they accept cutbacks or pay freezes. And so, following the latent competition among the various local tribal leaders for "a place under the sun," hatred evolves, which creates blindness and ignorance about what is happening in other public sectors in addition to the inability to grasp the depth and scope of the problem throughout the country as a whole.

---

67 The *Mizrachi* is the name of the religious Zionist organization founded in 1902. In 1956 the Mizrachi party and Hapoel HaMizrachi merged to form the National Religious Party to advance the rights of religious Jews in Israel, having fought the 1955 election together as the National Religious Front. The party was an ever-present government coalition member until 1992. In 2008 the party merged into the Jewish Home, essentially a successor party. (Wikipedia, s.v. "Mizrachi (religious Zionism)," last modified February 12, 2014, https://en.wikipedia.org/wiki/Mizrachi_(religious_Zionism))

That is to say, precisely when an internal unity in an internal political struggle is needed, the leaders can be possibly blinded to the comprehensive perception that might be important for their own survival as well as to the survival of the Israeli state.

Potential Resolutions

The two examples given in this brief chapter concern cultural product; therefore, it is possible to envision that this product may be corrected by a new public culture that will permeate the old one and replace it. This would require both the understanding of the public, which would be asked to change its views, as well as the understanding of the leadership, which would need to comprehend that on a road of hatred and lies, the state and/or the organization it is leading has no life expectancy. This is a demand to "change the channel," and it includes the utmost investment in open public relations accompanied by profound education, requiring a few years of waiting before the initial results may be gained.

After such input is given, I do hope that within one generation we will be able to exterminate this systemic failure and intensify the systems of the modern state and its social texture.

CHAPTER 6:

POSSIBLE SOLUTIONS

Touching the Three Bases

The truth is rarely pure and never simple.
—*Oscar Wilde*, **The Importance of Being Earnest: A Trivial Comedy for Serious People**

Introduction

This book cannot be finished before I suggest some possible solutions for the points I have brought up in the previous chapters. I wrote these essays over the course of a few months toward the end of 2013 and the beginning of 2014, and I completed many of them with narrow solutions for the problems that were pointed out. However, now the time has come to reflect on the situation in general and point out some inclusive solutions with an emphasis on the issue of a possible target.

Because I intend to examine solutions, I must separate the wheat from the chaff. That is why I concentrated on major solutions only. After these are implemented, it would also be possible to execute all the amendments that may be required later on. I have attached a list of some suggested amendments in Appendix B. However, to begin with, let's start with the first solution for Israel's social woes.

The First Social Solution: Strengthen the Community

As a conservative and Zionist, the Jewish state is an institutionalized value in my world just as the Declaration of Independence by the American founding fathers has justly gained its dwelling in the hearts of all those who love freedom and justice, wherever they are. Just like the spirit of American liberty, the spirit of Zionism was established by a few who boldly led continuous and concentrated community effort. Just as you cannot fathom the consolidation of the American concept without the dispersed and heterogeneous community structure of the American colonies, you also cannot describe the Zionistic idea without the comprehension of the representatives of the Zionist communities and federations that constituted the first Zionistic Congress.[68] Later on, these evolved into movements that afterward acted as the council's delegates.[69] For the individual who leads or the one who is led, there are always considerations of profit and loss, yet my Zionism is not based on personal earnings or loses.

Again, as a conservative, the value of the local communities is important, and it is a rising factor in my thinking. I perceive the community's medium- and small-sized businesses as the basis and foundation

---

68   The First Zionist Congress was the inaugural congress of the Zionist Organization (ZO) held in Basel (Basle), Switzerland, from August 29 to August 31, 1897. It was convened and chaired by Theodor Herzl, the founder of the modern Zionism movement. The Congress formulated a Zionist platform, known as the Basel program, and founded the Zionist Organization. The Congress was attended by some two hundred participants from seventeen countries, sixty-nine of whom were delegates from various Zionist societies, and the remainder were individual invitees. Ten non-Jews were also in attendance and were expected to abstain from voting. Seventeen women attended the Congress, some of them in their own capacity, others accompanying representatives. (Wikipedia, s.v. "First Zionist Congress," last modified July 26, 2015, https://en.wikipedia.org/wiki/First_Zionist_Congress)

69   The Zionist movement was produced by various philosophers representing different approaches concerning the objective and path that Zionism should follow. The principal common goal was the aspiration to establish a national home for the Jewish people. However, the method of action needed was in dispute. (Wikipedia, s.v. "Types of Zionism," last modified November 15, 2014, https://en.wikipedia.org/wiki/Types_of_Zionism) For more information, see Appendix A.

for the strength of the community and the intensification of the middle class. The power of the community is the one that can restrain and balance the power of the international corporation. The vitality of the community will balance the passion for power and wealth among the people of fortune and authority.

Yet, what is the actual meaning gained through the suggested reinforcement of the community?

First and foremost, it concerns the powers of local government, which should be increased. This increase should begin with the statutory strengthening and continue with the intensification of local educational values. The role of the mayor is one that requires following local law and keeping order; hence, the need for mayors to supervise their local police forces. This department should know how to handle local crime while following the rules of the community. In my vision, it is the same local force which at the same time follows the required national law and obeys the authority of the national units, as determined by the nationwide legislation. Of course, in order to preserve the equilibrium of the local powers, there is a need to elect local judges to balance and transfer power into the hands of the local committees/public, who should elect the magistrates in each area and settlements. All of this should be done on the basis of national criteria that would be observed professionally by the national legal system. The advantages of such community choices are ample since these may result in a variety of judiciary viewpoints for the legal system in its highest instances. This will prevent questions about whether the judiciary system is stagnant or its judges monolithic, for it will be clear that suggested local changes together with present processes will impact the promotion of judges and new judicial approaches.

I also suggest increasing the scope of the legislation that city and settlement councils are empowered to enact. This would create a constitutional barricade to block the power of the local executive authority. In such a world of values, each citizen has an impact on the composition of his or her community and hence, tighter relations with the community different establishment, participation in the election processes, and protest when it is required. It will lead each citizen to express his positions through local communication means.

Each owner of a medium-sized business would be able to affect the values of the community and thus his or her own economic existence during competition with the giant corporations. In addition, legal option will be given to local residents to establish community businesses as cooperative ones. Such businesses lower the mediation costs and act as proper competition for the bigger businesses.

In big cities, the neighborhood or quarter committee will act as the vanguard against the increasing power of City Hall and it will act as a catalyst for important borough developments. The clear reason for that is that the growing size obscures the connection between the actions of the individual and the reaction of the group. Group solidarity tends to crack when it contains too many individuals with different opinions, values and social backgrounds. Therefore, after the reference group in the community is too big, like in a growing town, there is a need to be on guard. If it grows above a certain limit, there is a need to break or divide this growing community into smaller segments that are more manageable in their human dimensions and allow each individual to have minimal impact on most of the other segments' residents.

In my view, the intensification of the community also would involve forming a second national house of representatives in addition to the "all state" Knesset.[70] This new house would be based on the local di-

---

70 The *Knesset* is the unicameral national legislature of Israel. As the legislative branch of the Israeli government, the Knesset passes all laws, elects the president and prime minister (although the latter is ceremonially appointed by the president), approves the cabinet, and supervises the work of the government. In addition, the Knesset elects the state comptroller. It also has the power to waive the immunity of its members, remove the president and the state comptroller from office, dissolve the government in a constructive vote of no confidence, and to dissolve itself and call new elections. The prime minister may dissolve the Knesset. However, until an election is completed, the Knesset maintains authority in its current composition. (Wikipedia, s.v. "Knesset," last modified July 28, 2015, https://en.wikipedia.org/wiki/Knesset)

vision. Perhaps it may seem an unnecessary expenditure, but in my humble opinion, the state of Israel could not complement its political maturation process without forming a secondary power focus, based on regional powers and community representation.

Even if this house of representatives is given the power to handle only issues of internal affairs, society, and economy, still its presence is needed to act as a tangible block against the national connections between the wealthy and the authority, which ignore the needs of the various local communities. That is to say that the relative wealth of the state budget and private investments would be divided among more areas, according to the requirements of the new political order that would be formed and that would require the confirmation of both houses of representatives regarding any legislation concerning issues affecting local economy and society. The representative for each community would be elected separately by the community members, based on their ideas and free will, which would prevent additional impact of outside influences on the community's considerations. In addition, this system would require the local press to use its power to aggressively review candidates and issues, and this scrutiny could be used as a tool in the hands of the citizens who aim to measure the nature of their delegates, heads of local councils and court judges.

All the above is in a sense a statutory intensification that may help prevent the needs of the individual from being subjugated to the needs of the rich minority who hold the power and erase the natural creative spirit and being of each community. For any place in which a person can have an impact becomes more satisfying when individuals realize that they have increased power to affect, to change or not to change, as they see fit.

Yet, what about the perceptions of the community's values as ones that defend the individual against the tyranny of the majority and as fortified barricade against the wealthy taking over most of the power points of the national system? This is where the education granted in the communities is going to gain its expression. Indeed, in my proposal, the community's education system will be accompanied by national supervision through core curriculum studies[71]—as it is done at present—but with the addition of community studies that will not cover more than 10 percent of the studying materials and hours. This addition, combined with the current curriculum that allows parental impact (presently within the permitted additional studies framework—up to 15 percent of the class lesson) will grant the community the possibility to define itself regarding levels of values and their educational translation as well as to form educational ethical obstructions among its graduates against any brain wash that comes with the media influence of wealthy and powerful corporations. The latter will also stop the deep penetration of unwanted values and ideas gained through elements with ample resources and craving power.

There are several benefits to granting communities the valuable power to determine, through their local educational committees and parents' committees, the actual part (approximately a quarter) of the curriculum that concerns the mutual community's values. It shapes and strengthens the coherence in the community, and it improves the individual's connections with the society in his or her residential area.

The significance of local autonomy goes much more than that. You can't get real social stability by dictating national rules upon different local populations. If what we look for is long-lasting social stability, then the regulations in many aspects of life should come as close to the ruts as possible. This is especially true if the diversity among the state local communities is so big that it means reaching a different status quo for each constituency. From the state point of view, releasing power to the local authorities gives social stability all over the land with less federal expenses.

---

71 *Core curriculum* is a program formulated by the Israeli ministry of education in which courses in mathematics, English, civics and basic computer skills are designed to serve as a common basis for all primary education institutions, with the stipulation that stats financial support be provided for implementation of these studies. This program was especially designed to give Haredi Yeshiva boys an elementary boarding ticket to the contemporary employment world.

This local empowerment by the state enables issues of faith to surface and be shaped within the national thinking system, too, without the need for input by a separate national political party This means that community values with faith characteristics may, from now on, surface at power cores to reach the national level at the house of representatives, which is based on regional representation, without the need for individual citizens to belong to a National Religious party, but as part of their entire community's values. This may also lead to ethical proximity between believers of various religions and those who are secular. This is a good example of how religious disputes could be mediated at the national level, through interreligious identity sharing the same values in the same local area, without the need for different definition of national political party. Consequently, at the end of the linking process, it may be assumed that the perceptions and values of the Bney-Braq community representatives at the regional house of representatives will partly overlap with the perceptions and values of the religious Muslim population in Umm al-Fahm or and the Christian one in Nazareth.[72] This will lead to cooperation between their delegates on the national level. This is yet another possible intensification of the local and eventually national values opposite the religious extremism in the area. This fringe behavior of religious extremism is rooted in global and nationwide movements that do not take into account the ideological or practical demands in the field (e.g., the will of their local communities and residents), which eventually is the reason why these groups allow themselves to be more extreme in their ideological messages.

---

72 Bney Brak is a city located on Israel's central Mediterranean coastal plain, just east of Tel Aviv, in the Dan metropolitan region and Tel Aviv district. Bney-Brak is a center of ultraorthodox (Haredi) Judaism. (Wikipedia, s.v. "Bney Brak," last modified July 18, 2015, https://en.wikipedia.org/wiki/Bnei_Brak) Umm al-Fahm is an Arabic city that is located twenty kilometers northwest of Jenin in the Haifa District of Israel with a population of 48,500, nearly all of whom are Arab citizens of Israel. Overlooking Wadi Ara, Umm al-Fahm is the social, cultural, and economic center for residents of the Wadi Ara and Triangle regions. (Wikipedia, s.v. "Umm al-Fahm," last modified July 13, 2015, https://en.wikipedia.org/wiki/Umm_al-Fahm)

**The Second Solution—the Economic One: Temporarily Suspend
Pension Savings**

For most of us, the major fear is that of the unknown. That is why we save
for our old age. We do not know what our fate will be. Will we age slowly
and with dignity, without complicated illnesses and heavy costs? Or perhaps will we die young and abruptly? One way or another, the pension
we are saving, either in the form of a fund or through investments, is
supposed to cope with a substantial part of our old age.

Following the current actuarial calculations, it is clear and certain
for all savers in Israel that there is a time bomb on their doorstep. The
pension savings of most savers in Israel will not provide even the smallest
part of their future demands. In fact, already today, it may be asserted
that an entire generation of people aged forty to forty-five and younger
are doomed to a life of poverty and meagerness at their old age. This
will leave their children's generation with the dilemma: should they help
their aging parents or their own families? In the future, this situation
may, in my humble opinion, increase the social tensions up to the point
of breakdown.

The economic reasons for this state are clear. There are the high
management fees, which stem from the lack of true competition in the
market. There is an absence of effective, governmental regulation, due
to the relationship between the wealthy and the authorities that ensures
that people in the high governmental administration have work offers
until and after retirement at the biggest financial corporations that were
previously under their supervision. For members of the upper circles,
there is the availability of loans based upon pension finances that more
than often do not have to be repaid. These lost loans affect the sum value of pensions for all the investors. Medical developments prolong old
age, and hence there has been a decline in the percentage of the young
who carry the burden of work (in some cases, added to the burden of
supporting through ones parents personal savings because of the higher
costs—which increase each year—to bring up a child in each family).
In addition, the required annual growth of investments is often not met

due to global catastrophes that are not controlled by the governments or by individuals, all these circumstances and many others have led to a bleak horizon for all those who save.

In order to cope with such uncertainty, there is a need to think outside the box without necessary reference to existing tools. However, as a conservative, I do suggest relying on historical cases with proven success. My suggestion in this case is to temporarily cancel the pension institute and instead temporarily introduce community care for the elderly as part of communal duty in addition to that of the state for each citizen.

To provide community care, on the one hand, a national service is needed in which young people helped the local families in need. On the other hand, massive building (which would also contribute to the advancement of the economy) is also needed in order to provide shelter for golden-age people. In parallel, seniors would be included within the community and local budgeting with some state governmental support, which would all lead to the intensification of the community's relations. My proposed system of community care would also strengthen citizens' confidence in the stability of their relations with the state of Israel and in their ability to survive with dignity.

Of course, in order to prevent unwanted expenses, capital and assets thresholds would be determined for retirees participating in this program - anything above that level would either decrease the support or annul it completely. There would be the lucky ones who could choose between private accommodation and other options that are open for them, but all the rest would gain basic dimensions of human respect at their old age. In addition, all young people would know that if, and only if, for reasons unrelated to them, they did not make enough money or save for pension funds in their lives, they could be assured that they would not be left out on the street in old age.

In parallel, regulatory and other amendments to the existing and future pension funds would be conducted following the requirements of the actuarial calculations. Obviously, it may take some time to refill the corrected retirement accounts and to determine how best to structure savings without having to worry about future political involvement, but my plan would still have a more successful regulation basis. Some percentage of the pension funds and savings of those who are economically strong would be transferred to the state and local authorities during that intermediate period. For a predetermined short period, the state and local goverment would provide the services required for all its citizens whereas some of these finances—especially of the less-financially-secure citizens—would be left in their hands to be used to support their families.

This idea is based morally on the basic biblical decree "Honor thy father and thy mother" (Exodus 20:12) and also on some fundamental verses such as "Cast me not off in the time of old age; forsake me not when my strength fails" (Psalms 71:9).

These quotations are not meant to encourage parasites, for most people do save for the proverbial rainy day. The question is: how long can they hang onto their savings? What is the economic value of the social unrest that stems from the slow starvation of many of the current parental generation, people who are now in their mid-forties and below? Members of this generation are saving, but they already know that they will never gain the promise that is supposedly embodied in these savings.

Another advantage in this approach to housing retirees in separate safe homes is that thousands of apartments that were populated by the elderly would become available. These apartments would enter the rent and sales market and lead the Israel housing market toward relaxation, which would alleviate the housing distress found in the younger generation a little.

Once again, I wish to stress the fact that I am not advocating changing over to a socialistic economy and certainly not a communist one. Still, until we fix the capitalistic economy's mechanisms, we will have to deal (for the sake of social stability) with one or two generations who are waiting for a structured, systemic answer. These people believed and still do in the free market method, but the centralization of the capital in the hands of the super corporations and the political power of the members of that upper social class created a situation in which a biased market has robbed their savings. My claim is that if we do not wish to withdraw completely from the free market, it is best for us to take one calculated step backward and ensure the future of one or two generations while we handle the required amendments in our pension savings and thus gain social peace and political relaxation, which would also affect the economic stability.

Perhaps in such cases, the capital owners would pay more than their required share, but in fact, they would also protect their status and assets from instability and from a social environment that could easily turn into a revolutionary one. President Franklin Roosevelt took a similar action during the New Deal days to overcome the failure of the regulation and the loss of the road to the free market. What was suitable during the greatest economic depression the world has ever known is sevenfold as suitable in our times when we are trying to prevent the actualization of a crisis.

To the best of my understanding, a unique mutual interest can evolve here in Israel between the capital owners and the politicians, together with the average citizens, in the success of such an all-inclusive move.

The Third Solution—Faith: Separate Religious Practice from the State
So far, I have referred to a pair of solutions, permanent and temporary, aimed at stabilizing the social and economic situation in the country: namely, a solution for each discipline. Now, I want to describe another necessary solution, which stems from the spiritual direction. My understanding is that in order to lower the pressure of interreligious confrontation, there should be separation between the daily mechanisms and the individual perceptions of faith by members in society. We must leave the issue of whether each religion has the ability to reach a compromise, since by nature their dogmatic institutions are not prone to yielding; this illusive capability (to compromise) must be left for the greater national

issues. At the local arena, preventing daily friction on the basis of faith would contribute to the decrease of the tension that builds up through the structured conflicts in the state of Israel, not only in the Palestinian-Jewish confrontations but also in secular-religious confrontations.

The way I see it, there is a need to hold a big conference with the participation of representatives from all religious councils. The goal would be to separate the religious sphere of conduct from the national arena where it is presently situated and where it dictates by law the conduct of all citizens in daily life. Under the suggested arrangement, the citizens would not be required to adhere to any kind of religious rule or conduct. The religious sphere of action needs the local community, and only that community is authorized to enact laws regarding these issues. Yet, even that should be done meticulously with consideration for the needs of the people who are not religious or who belong to a different religion and are living within the same area.

The big religious council I envision would consist of the important adjudicators and thinkers from the three major religions (Judaism, Christianity, and Islam), and it would handle principle questions regarding relations and tensions within the community and between ethnic groups. Its adjudications and decisions would not require the state's involvement; instead, these would be used as a tool for consultation and guidance for the members of the local councils, the parliament houses, and the public of believers.

The decisions of this council would be made only unanimously, which might require consent and perhaps compromise between all parties. The delegates for the council would be elected by the religious hierarchy in each faith and according to the relative part of the subdivisions in each faith relative to its required size (i.e., Sunni-Shiites, Hassidic-Lithuanian, Reform-Orthodox, Catholic-Protestant, Religious-Secular, and so on).

Decisions concerning the conduct rules at the residence place should be made within the community's framework. Preventing any form of personal worship based on any kind of religious decree should be totally prohibited, and the general character of the community's public sphere would be determined through the choice of the relevant local delegates. No status quo would be supervised nationally. Each settlement and each electoral district would choose the kinds of values its residents want to uphold. At the same time, each individual would be allowed to choose to practice his or her own values in his or her residence place based on his or her beliefs. That is to say that if religious people live within a secular area, they should be given a place in which to practice their ceremonies and rituals. This would be taken care of by the local council, which would see to the allocation of public areas for them based on the local and national legislation. The same is true for the opposite situation: secular people living in a religious Jewish area would be enabled to reach their houses, with their cars, on Saturdays or holidays. However, if, for example, the decision was made in any district to maintain zero tolerance regarding pictures exposing human bodies in the open public areas, everyone would have to abide by that rule.

That is to say, there would be a separation between the public domain, in which the local character is determined and salient, and the conduct of the individual, which requires protection of his or her basic rights (free prayers and free movement all year round).

The purpose for this separation would be to increase tolerance and help individuals to be connected into a larger public. Instead having discussions imposed by national and multinational parties, discussions would concern the evolving local values and their relative importance. This kind of conversation would hopefully help to block the spread of national greed and avarice, and, one may hope, also block extremism. In addition, it would enhance the local communities and their moral unity. Moreover, housing areas 'look and feel' would be the most similar to the inhabitants' wants, without imposing on individuals or minorities.

Marriage, divorce, burial, and birth are indeed in the interest of the individual within the community, so a national assembly should not dictate the form of faith or life to anyone. It may be permitted in communist countries or dictatorships, but not in a state called "A light unto the nations," which the classic Zionism based on the road of Ahad Haam aspired to establish.

The Jewish religious community may amply benefit from taking such steps as I am recommending. On the one hand, its freedom of action would grow once it was no longer under the supervision of the state, while on the other hand, it would be possible to make much-needed reforms of its conduct and orientation. This community would rise above its level of mediocrity in education and occupational attainment, and it *would* develop, for it does have the want for intellectual excellence, which characterized and still influences the Jewish communities around the world. On the other hand, after the issue of getting payments from the government for Yeshiva studying disappears, many would be free to acquire crafts and thus contribute to the improvement of their lifestyles and the production levels in the state in general. [73]

The religious Christian community would also flourish in such a situation, where it would be independent and not a minority "ward" among the Arab mainly Muslim congregations. The religious Muslims would gain their spiritual rights everywhere in the country, without discrimination, and secular individuals would finally be able to build around themselves the environment based on their perceptions where they can flourish.

For the first time in many decades, it would be possible for all citizens to express their way of life in their own unique way and contribute or not to their house of prayers and their religious needs without the involvement of the state in its budgeting, but through responsibility to their respected congregations and commitment to the minorities around them.

The perceptive reader must have noticed that I am not indicating a way to contradict the belief about the here-and-now coming of the

---

73 At present, the Israeli government allocates a progressive livelihood fee for each Yeshiva student, which might be lost if he goes to work. Moreover, under the Yeshiva educational system, you concentrate on studying religious material and nothing else.

Messiah, or the call for Jihad in the Muslim sector. This kind of remedy would require a long time and the establishment of excellent religious leadership as well as deepening the education on issues regarding values and faith. All these combined with history studies, as a live and breathing symbol, would hopefully provide the Israeli state with the immunization it needs in order to cope with the self-governability of the Jewish people for the first time in two thousand years and amid the currently stormy torrents of the neighboring Islamic world.

CHAPTER 7:

THE ELEPHANT IN THE CHINA SHOP

*Thoughts about Possible and Different Solutions
for the Israeli-Palestinian Conflict*

All war is a symptom of man's failure as a thinking animal.
—John Steinbeck, **Once There Was a War**

It is difficult to live in the state of Israel without being conscious of the biggest conflict that is bubbling within it. It is sevenfold times as hard to attempt to solve economic and social problems in this situation, which is very much entangled in the lives of the two publics.

In this chapter, I am not even attempting to examine whether there is a long history to the Palestinian people or how much justice there is in the "preaching" of their leaders. I accept the fact as it was well expressed in a famous Israeli song, "Suddenly a man gets up in the morning and feels that he is a nation and starts walking"[74]

Henceforth, it is the duty of each one of us to think about a solution. When I think of a possible way out, I do not think about absolute justice or a situation in which each party can achieve all that is due to it based on this or that viewpoint in history. Actually, in my opinion, the past has no meaning, if its entire role is to cause social unrest in the present as basis for destruction of the future. The conservative within me refuses

---

74 Opening words of a famous Israeli song written by the poet Amir Gilboa (born 25 September 1917 - died 2 September 1984)

to accept revolutions and social oscillations that cause the utmost suffering to one party or even to both parties, as I do understand that such a situation may only lead to lack of peace for the two publics: the Jewish and the Palestinian.

In my attempt to examine the existing situation, I am inclined to think that for many reasons, the lives of the two nations are interwoven without any possibility of separating the two. Economically, the Palestinian people rely on the economy constructed by the Jewish folk throughout the years in which it built its homeland. The entire Palestinian work structure is oriented toward the State of Israel and not its other neighboring countries. The economic structure regarding the sources of water, gas, and energy products also relies on the Israeli economy. The local resident in the areas of Judea, Samaria and the Gaza Strip tend to value the shekel (NIS) as a strong currency that buys and sells in their markets as well. When these residents work for the Jews, their salaries are paid in NIS, and the entire monetary system of the Palestinian Authority also relies—among other things—on the Israeli customs and taxation system. There are thousands of workers who leave their area daily to find their breadwinning on the Israeli/Jewish side of the border, either within the world-recognized area of the state of Israel or in the industrial zones that were founded alongside Jewish settlements in Judea and Samaria.

The geography of residential areas and the places providing jobs and employment for both nations is also mixed. In fact, except for the Gaza Strip, there is no clear, continuous line of a simple geometric form on the map of Israel that provides a settlement and work area that clearly belongs to one nation only. Any attempt to form this kind of area requires special angles and projections and obviously a few additional corrections that will turn the sketched line into a procedural nightmare regarding its defense and policing management.

An overview seems to indicate that it is extremely difficult, if not impossible, to create two states with homogeneous populations on both sides of the border. In many ways, this situation is the same as the situation in many European and other countries around the world. For example, regardless of the history concerning the conflict between the French and Germans, there is a wide strip of land involving people from the two nations on both sides of the border. Similarly, it is possible to see that despite the difficult conflicts that evolved between the Hindus and the Muslims, the foundation of Pakistan and Bangladesh did not prevent Muslims and Hindus to live side by side within India. Hence, the solution for two independent nations is not necessarily achieved by keeping a distinct and homogenous area completely free of all members from the other nation.

When borderlines are outlined around the world, it is common to accept the fact that some minorities from the neighboring country remain in their places regardless of the position of the border lines. This is true whether it is a folk-related minority or an ethnic group (e.g., Shiites or Sunni). I have no doubt that in the existing conflict between Jews and Palestinians there is a need to admit that minorities—of this or that magnitude—would have to remain on the other side of the border. Any other probability might lead to social stress and grave restlessness that, during the process, would eventually penetrate the neighboring country, either through economic means or through war and terror. Peace between the two nations necessitates recognizing the right of the two publics to remain in their present privately owned lands while a political layout is being built that is based on the existing construction processes on the disputed ground. Again, as a conservative I do see the importance of developing processes based on existing facts rather than using parachute solutions that would cause trauma following evacuation and detachment of people on both sides of the border. Consequently, it would be essential to have mutual recognition of all the settlements (the formally acknowledged and the unacknowledged, the Palestinian and the Jewish ones) on both sides of the border—excluding those about which there is consensus regarding the need to change their location. The latter decision may be based on environmental or other factors considered to be extensive and concerning the health of the residents.

The question is how do we neutralize the friction between the majority and the minority? This question is especially thorny when considering matters concerning the moral national decisions made on each side that enrage or ignite anger among the minorities who feel persecuted or treated as outcasts due to their national difference.

Following my decision to try to solve this challenge, and for lack of other possibilities, I turned to the example that seemed the closest—that of Switzerland. In fact, this country consists of a confederate structure of nations and areas of land. Switzerland has maintained a subtle balance among the disparate lands, enabling preservation of the people's separatism while producing advantages through the economic-geographic mixture and creating one big, cooperating, and functioning state. I am not the first to turn in that direction for comparisons, but in my case, I did add another link concerning the actualization of the local rights for each inhabitant.

The local conflict in the Holy Land differs in many key areas from the one in the Swiss cantons. As such, it requires a different sort of problem solving, and the solution needs to fit the dimensions of the local arena and its participants with their different characters and behaviors. The major goal is to turn the areas of Judea, Samaria, and maybe even the Gaza Strip into one canton and the rest of the Israeli areas into the other canton. When I say "canton," I am referring to a political division that is modeled somewhat on the states that are members of the American federation but with far greater independence and decision-making abilities on the local state level. The power of the two suggested cantons should be roughly like the power of a state in the European community but with some added federal limitations.

These states would sanctify the existing status quo regarding settlements or dwellings in the area except for the required, minor changes. In fact, the peace treaty between them would be the first agreement in a series of obligatory agreements that would be signed, successively, within a short period of time and would be ratified by their individual parliaments and the people. The main purpose of these agreements

would be to create a confederation that would integrate the foreign affairs policy, the inner state and outfacing security measures, and specific economic aspects such as customs and monetary policies into a
compelling confederate structure. The goal would be to form a body
that is managed by the two nations through full mutual consent. Both
countries would maintain separate rule of their citizens and issue separate legislation except regarding issues that need to be addressed by
the confederacy. The confederate government as well as its high judicial system will consist of an equal number of delegates elected by their
political colleagues in the corresponding parliaments of the two sides
(Palestinian and Israeli). In the joint confederate parliament, an equal
number of seats will be allocated corresponding to the division of the
partnering nations, since these delegates will be elected by their people
on both sides of the border.

The minorities in each state will vote for the local authorities in the
area where they live but not for the state's authorities. Each minority
member will be entitled to all the rights existing in the state where he or
she lives, excluding voting for state political institutes. On election day,
minority members may vote for the political institutes of their people,
much as a Norwegian in the European community who lives in Britain
and wants to vote for the Norwegian parliament is allowed to vote in
Norwegian elections. The Norwegian may vote at the relevant embassy
or at any other appointed place designated by Norwegian law for citizens wanting to vote abroad; however, he or she cannot vote for representation in the British Parliament.

Now, turn from this example to the imagined reality in Israel. On
election day, minority members would be able to vote for the parliament
in their countries of origin beyond their immediate canton's/country's
border. In addition, they would also vote for local delegates in the local
community where they actually live.

On the one hand, this kind of solution would strengthen the involvement of minority members in the issues of the local community where
they live and from which they draw the source of their power and part

of their personal identity. On the other hand, while not losing any of their civilian rights, they would gain the right to vote in national elections and could cast their votes on the side of their people. In this case there would be separation between the individual's need for national and political definition that contains the element of self-definition, and the need for community involvement and the continuation of daily life with protection of the individual's current rights. That is to say that the individual's autonomy would be protected on the nationally defined level as a Palestinian or a Israeli, as well as on the local level as a citizen with equal rights, like all the others, regardless of his affiliation with a minority group in the territory where he lives.

This solution would also prevent the perpetual friction that arise when minorities vote on national or popular matters and supposedly prevent the majority from achieving its popular, national goals due to the impact of the minority on the national political balance.

The Jewish and Palestinian cantons would confront social and cultural issues that have a reciprocal impact on the two states. If there is a need for full consensus about procedural matters regarding any change in foreign policy, security, monetary policy, or taxation, then this would require an agreed-upon compromise, which in turn, would further strengthen the culture of political concessions between the two states. In addition, any other cultural or social need that was decided in one state would permeate clearly through the minority on the other side of the border into the other state's cultural and social realm. For example, any legislation concerning one minority will immediately cross the state's border and influence the local legislators in the other state.

Can the two nations accept this kind of solution? This depends on the maturation level of the conflict and on the data regarding foreign impacts from various sources. I do not even know if this is the solution that will be implemented, but undoubtedly, it is relevant to the needs and fears of both parties. This solution does not address the concerns of those who advocate for the right of return, because the Palestinian who wants to live within the boundaries of Israel will not be able to have an impact on the national elections. Still, on the local level, he or she may have a connection with the community and the ability to make political, economic, and cultural impacts.

Under my plan, Jewish settlers would not be uprooted from their land, and their links with the mother-state would be protected through their ability to vote for their national and confederative institutions. Nevertheless, they would present no threat to the Palestinian nationality or its natural development.

The two nations could enjoy the mutual framework that would grant each citizen from one of the states the same civil rights as he or she has in the state where he or she lives (excluding national voting). On the other hand, all his or her economic business and work life could be conducted on both sides of the border through integration and reciprocity, which, in turn, would enhance the power of the economy and society in which he or she lives.

The future holds the solutions, but there is no doubt that any situation that does not include a permanent solution for this conflict will force each side to pay an economic, social and cultural price. I can only hope that the solution—whatever it is—will be reached soon.

CHAPTER 8:

AND WHAT IF...

*I shall be telling this with a sigh
    Somewhere ages and ages hence:
Two roads diverged in a wood, and I,
I took the one less traveled by,
And that has made all the difference."*
—Robert Frost, The Road Not Taken

I wrote this book during a stormy period in the Arab world, which is torn between the reformists and the clergy and between the Shiites and the Sunnis. This situation is one of increasing extremism and violence due to reasons relating to ethnic origin or tribal issues. The book was also written following the growing and intensifying social awareness of the deficiencies in existing methods and the increase hostility of most of the Israeli public toward its political and economic leaders.

In view of these circumstances, I must always consider my suggested solutions carefully: perhaps they are inapplicable or unacceptable or uncommon. If so, what road should be taken?

Prophesy has long vanished from Israel—ever since the Temple was destroyed. Nevertheless, there is a need to prepare for various scenarios, including extremist ones. Undoubtedly, since the events of summer 2011, weighty social and economic factors were included, for the first time, within the calculations of social and government stability in Israel. Can the aggregation of problems and failures create an extreme situation that will lead to the fall of the Israeli state? Perhaps, In such a case, there would be a need to verify the abilities and wants of the Jewish communities in the world to become involved and to absorb Jewish refugees from the once-was state. yet I do not think this scenario is likely.

I am more perturbed by the possibility of change in the ruling methods of our government that may lead to a rise of extremism in tyrannical levels. These extremists might take actions that would be very difficult to atone for. One must never disregard causes of extremism and their ability to capture the hearts of the nation in times of trouble and distress. The social and political events that just recently took place in Greece are a gruesome reminder for just that. The price to be paid if we allowed extremism to triumph would persecute the Jewish nation to its last day.

A revolution by the masses is not a cause for "having a party," but rather a source of profound concern. In the Israeli case, it could be related to a state with top of the region military capabilities, and according to some whispers, all kinds of judgment-day weapons. I am not trying to assume what the results of the French Revolution could have been had the Jacobeans acquired some kind of chemical or biological formula that would have granted them judgment-day weapons to be used against their enemies. Thoughts about the "could have been" are quite atrocious.

Zionism is a legitimate national movement of the Jewish people. Each national movement that was founded and established the boundaries of the motherland during the twentieth century suffered from various kinds of illnesses in the course of its development and until its mission was completed. The same is true of Zionism, but its main goal was and still is to determine a motherland with acceptable borders for the Jewish people in a region where their ancestors had deep roots.

From the outset, being pragmatic and seeing reality were essential parts of what the Jews were doing in the land of Israel, and the belief that the Arabs were citizens with equal rights and duties was anchored in its Declaration of Independence. However, due to human nature and the failures of the system, these points were not actually integrated. One must not direct complaints at the previous generation but rather recognize that just as in all national movements, at the extremes of Zionism there are the ultranationalists and the extreme anarchists who keep "attacking the rear" and bickering without mercy. Added to that, there is an inner dissatisfaction that is spreading among the masses in Israel, and that is expressed through political instability and migration out of the country by those who can afford it. When this dissatisfaction is combined with the external and internal hatred of Israel by some of the Palestinian people, then it seems that there becomes a problematic formula. This formula distorts the view of the leadership and the public, and prevents the Israeli state from achieving its goals without costing citizens their rights.

Poor children have the right to a respectable existence as long as their parents are able to make the most of their given ability. Workers have the right to fair payment in exchange for their toil, as long as their place of employment is not harmed. Rich people have a right to their property as long as it is not part of the state's treasury, in which case it would belong to all its citizens. Believers have a right to practice their faith as long as their practice respects their neighbors. It is the right of Jews and Palestinians to be citizens with equal rights in the new Israeli nation, as long as the state is acknowledged as refuge and national home for the Jewish people without harming, even a little, the rights and duties of the Israeli-Palestinian citizens.

Whether an investor, businessman, or a state representative, it is recommended for large corporations to invest in Israel. But the fact that Israelis welcome large foreign investments doesn't necessarily mean that they should be afraid to stand against the bullying of rich and influential people. Around the world people should hear the Israeli cry: "Not everything that comes with fortune is welcomed here, especially if it has some detrimental effect on our basic values as a society and as individuals."

The utmost-argent task of the present time would be, in my eyes, to rebuild the Israeli elite. This new elite, while consolidating the new set of social and political rules, should be a model for the rest of the nation as well and should help to lead the country to safer shores.

...But, if you do not wish it, all this that I have related to you is and will remain a fable
—*Theodor Herzl,* **Altneuland (Old-New Land)**[75]

❧

---

75 In this 1902 work, which was written as a novel, Herzl observes the events in the lifespan of the Jewish nation in the state that will be established in the future. He calls for the development of the land using science and technology, and he advocates patience and tolerance in all endeavors, including in relations between the Arab and Jewish populations in the land of Israel. In *Old-New Land,* Herzl expresses his desire to organize the society according to the principle of mutual solidarity. The motto of the book that is quoted here has become the slogan of the Zionist movement.

MORE ABOUT VARIOUS SIDES OF ZIONISM[76]

*The **Zionist Movement** was produced by various philosophers representing different approaches concerning the objective and path that Zionism should follow. The principal common goal was the aspiration to establish a national home for the Jewish people. However, the method of action needed was in dispute. There were two main approaches to the modus operandi:*

- **Political Zionism**: Led by Theodor Herzl and Max Nordau in Russia. This Zionist organization approach espoused at the First Zionist Congress aimed to establish for the Jewish people a publicly and legally assured home in Palestine because it encompassed an area of Jewish religious culture. Among other items, the movement included initial steps to obtain governmental grants from the established powers that controlled the area.

- **Practical Zionism**: Led by Moshe Leib Lilienblum and Leon Pinsker and molded by the Hovevei Zion organization. This approach opined that firstly there was a need in practical terms to implement Jewish immigration to the land of Israel, Aliyah, and to settle the land as soon as possible, even if a charter over the land was not obtained.

---

76 This Appendix is based upon (Wikipedia, s.v. "Types of Zionism," last modified November 15, 2014, https://en.wikipedia.org/wiki/Types_of_Zionism.)

Later on, a combination of these two main approaches was produced:

- **Synthetic Zionism**: Led by Chaim Weizmann, Leo Motzkin and Nahum Sokolow, an approach that advocated a combination of the preceding two approaches. Another division between these generic types of Zionism derives from ideological differences that do not necessarily have to do with Zionism itself, but rather a comprehensive world view held by the people of these different groups regarding the character of the future Jewish state.

Another division between these generic types of Zionism derives from ideological differences that do not necessarily have to do with Zionism itself, but rather a comprehensive world view held by the people of these different groups regarding the character of the future Jewish State:

- **Labor Zionism:** as opposed to Practical and Political Zionism, Labor Zionism desired to establish an agriculturist society not on the basis of a private bourgeoisie society, but rather on the basis of moral equality.
- **Revisionist Zionism:** Revisionist Zionism was initially led by Ze'ev Jabotinsky and later by his successor, Menachem Begin (later prime minister of Israel), and emphasized the romantic elements of Jewish nationality, and the historical heritage of the Jewish people in the land of Israel as the constituent basis for the Zionist national idea and the establishment of the Jewish state. Followers of this movement supported liberalism and particularly economic liberalism, and opposed Labor Zionism and the establishing of a communist society in the land of Israel. Revisionist Zionism opposed any containment of Arab terror and supported firm military action against the Arab gangs that had attacked the Jewish community in the land of Israel. Due to that position, a faction of the Revisionist leadership split from that movement in order to establish the underground Irgun.

This group of people who split from the original movement is also categorized as supporters of Greater Israel.

- **Cultural Zionism:** cultural Zionism opined that the fulfillment of the national revival of the Jewish people should be achieved by creating a cultural center in the land of Israel and an educational center to the Jewish Diaspora, which together would be a bulwark against the danger of assimilation that threatens the existence of the Jewish people.

- **Revolutionary Zionism:** Revolutionary Zionism viewed Zionism as a revolutionary struggle to gather the Jewish exiles from the Diaspora together, revive the Hebrew language as a spoken vernacular, and reestablish a Jewish kingdom in the land of Israel. As members of Lehi during the 1940s, many adherents of Revolutionary Zionism engaged in guerilla warfare against the British administration in an effort to end the British Mandate of Palestine and pave the way for Jewish political independence. Following the state of Israel's establishment, leading figures of this movement argued that the creation of the state of Israel was never the goal of Zionism but rather a tool to be used in realizing the goal of Zionism, which they called *Malkhut Yisrael* (the Kingdom of Israel). Revolutionary Zionists are often mistakenly included among Revisionist Zionists but differ ideologically in several areas. Whereas Revisionists were for the most part secular nationalists who hoped to achieve a Jewish state that would exist as a commonwealth within the British Empire, Revolutionary Zionists advocated a form of national-messianic ideology that aspired toward a vast Jewish kingdom with a rebuilt temple in Jerusalem. Revolutionary Zionism generally espoused anti-imperialist political views and included both right-wing and left-wing nationalists among its adherents. Adherents of this movement are also categorized as supporters of Greater Israel.

- **Religious Zionism:** Religious Zionism maintained that both holding Jewish identity (which includes nationality) and establishing the state of Israel are religious duties derived from the Torah. As opposed to some members of the Jewish non-secular community, who claimed that the redemption of the land of Israel will occur only after the coming of the messiah, who will fulfill this aspiration, they maintained that human acts of redeeming the land will bring about the messiah, as their slogan states: *the land of Israel for the people of Israel according to the Torah of Israel.* Today they are commonly referred as the Religious Nationalists or the settlers, and are also categorized as supporters of Greater Israel.

THE WAY TOWARD REFORMS:
ADDITIONAL SUGGESTED CORRECTIONS

Economic Corrections

1. Eighty percent of encouragement and investment grants would be given only to small industries and micro businesses.
2. Building shopping malls in the city centers would not be allowed.
3. In each public and governmental tender, there will be a self-explanatory preference for the small trader if he can offer the same quality and price.
4. All students, from early kindergarten through college, would be educated about the need to save money.
5. The right of the Israeli government to govern its land on the highest possible level (through the National Land Law) would be declared, but privatization of most of the lots and lands would also be allowed. The Israeli Land Administration would be dismantled as the body that sells and divides land.
6. The whole country would be crisscrossed with high-speed computer lines and high-speed train lines.
7. Support for the elderly, the handicapped, and invalids would be expanded mainly through local untaxed charity initiatives to allow realistic survival.
8. Individual farmers would be given direct support, rather than receiving aid through economic or other specific councils or corporate farms.

9. The wage pyramid would be reversed by granting higher salaries to neighborhood police force, fire fighters, community doctors, district medical teams, local social workers, and teachers. A nice gesture would be to decrease the salaries of CEOs and deputy-director generals in public service by 10 percent through taxes. Another nice gesture would be for CEOs and deputy-director generals in the private market to voluntarily take pay cuts of a fixed percentage. The total of all those tax deductions could then be used to fund the salary increases for the newly preferred public servants (policemen, social workers, and so on).

Corrections in Education

1. Educating students about values, namely patience, tolerance, and recognition of the three major religions, would begin in the first grades in primary school.
2. Studies of Hebrew, Arabic, and Yiddish cultures would be compulsory in all schools.
3. Through community studies, students would learn about mutual support (charity, grace, and mercy).
4. Youth movements and youth centers would be required to address both cultural and religious diversity.
5. There would be a Nationwide program to raise the ambition for an elitist approach instead of the popular culture, internally and through school education.
6. Environmental studies (including the reciprocal relations between humans and nature and nature as a trust deposited in our hands) would be compulsory.
7. Studying some elected materials through rote memorization would be encouraged, but at the same time emphasis would be placed on studying through analytic and professional tools.

Political Corrections

1. The platforms of the political parties would combine culture and religion without any discrimination.
2. Religion would be separated from the national parliamentary legislation. The state is sovereign, and within its framework, there is freedom of religion and freedom from religion.
3. Racial discrimination would be severely punished with specific units and attorneys (prosecutors) for these issues.
4. The practice of reducing jail time by "one third for good behavior" would no longer be allowed for felonies involving racism and discrimination.
5. There would be direct and open elections for all parties during primaries. All parties would share with each other the same official list of voters to avoid duplication. The state would enable free primaries on the Internet for all candidates.
6. There would be indefinite restraining orders against racial slurs of any kind from the Knesset and any other governmental position.
7. Any abusive racial expression used by a person holding an elected public position would result in a reduction of 10 percent from the budget of the body represented by that person. That sum would be transferred to the body representing those who were hurt.
8. The legislation of the land laws (Israeli formal constitution) would be completed. The army would be turned into a national army of the state, and alongside it, there would be a professional standing army (with separate promotion tracks from the national army).

Social Corrections

1. Intercommunity relationships would be formed between the various religious communities that are geographically close.

2. Residential areas for individuals would be opened without distinguishing between the different religious and ethnic groups.

3. Employees would slowly purchase ownership of the press and local media. Tax benefits for local contributions aimed at supporting the local media would be granted to and in the relevant district.

4. The fit unemployed would be given a salary for doing public service work (e.g., repairs of roads and infrastructures).

5. Holidays of all religions would be acknowledged at institutions and government agencies. For example, the dates of vacation days and religious symbols would be posted at the entrances of all official bureaus.

6. It would be prohibited to disconnect electricity, water, or gas to people with disabilities, elderly people receiving nursing care, or terminally ill patients.

7. Conciliation committees would be established in neighboring settlements with hostile histories. Exposure of self-participation in illegal actions regarding hate crimes would be encouraged in a measured exchange for dismissal of self-incrimination.

8. National-service voluntary-support layouts shall be formed where they are most needed: nursing, the Red Star of David, *Zaka* (Hebrew for "Identification of Disaster Victims"), police patrol, and so on.

9. The whole population would be integrated through work and national service. (The sources of work and services would be open for all.)

www.ingramcontent.com/pod-product-compliance
Lightning Source LLC
Chambersburg PA
CBHW070146290526
45789CB00002B/651